"*Defying the Verdict* is a wonderful book: deeply human, full of ... and suffering. Full of the author's courage and faith. Charita Brown describes her bipolar illness in telling detail; her writing is powerful and eloquent. I highly recommend this book."

—KAY REDFIELD JAMISON, author of *An Unquiet Mind*

"Charita Cole Brown writes with grace, vulnerability, and a fearless urgency about being a black woman with bipolar disorder. Her story is remarkable, full of insight and inspiration."

—NANA-AMA DANQUAH, author of *Willow Weep For Me: A Black Woman's Journey Through Depression*

"In an artful and gripping account of life inside an over-imaginative brain, Charita's fierce determination to ride the waves of her illness with unshakeable resolve inspires fortitude in the most challenging of personal circumstances. Grounded by her family's love and her own undeniable intellect, this victorious story activates hope for those with and without a brain-based illness."

—CASSANDRA JOUBERT, author of *Losing Control: Loving A Black Child With Bipolar Disorder*

"Most people who buy a book about mental illness are seeking education. With style and grace *Defying the Verdict* does just that. But Charita Cole Brown's narrative also gives the reader a positive dose of hope and encouragement—just what the reader needs. Brown's account of her journey is straightforward, her symptoms carefully worded. Be open, don't hide. Her life is not easy, but she finds a way to exist in a dignified and satisfying manner. As a member of a family where mental illness is well known, I recommend this exceptional book."

—MIMI BAIRD, author of *He Wanted the Moon: The Madness and Medical Genius of Dr. Perry Baird and His Daughter's Quest to Know Him*

"We don't talk about mental illness—especially in African-America families! In *Defying the Verdict: My Bipolar Life*, Charita Cole Brown shares her arduous journey living through bipolar disorder. With honesty and in raw detail, Ms. Brown illustrates how genetics, childhood experiences, family dynamics, race and shame affect diagnosis and treatment. She eventually overcomes the intertwined obstacles and roadblocks along her path, demonstrating how to live your best life in the midst of a traumatic illness. It is a must read!"

—ANDREA M. COLE, Producer, *Opening Minds, Ending Stigma* documentary series

"In *Defying the Verdict*, Brown vividly presents a compelling story of her descent into and through the frightening depths and euphoric heights of Bipolar Disorder. She deftly plants the early seeds, within herself, and within her family, that later manifested in the full-blown disease that overtook her as a college student. It was then that her disease threatened to destroy her promising future.

Defying the Verdict underscores the notion that it is possible to not only survive a diagnosis of Bipolar Disorder but that one can live a full life and thrive. Brown's book is a document of the strength, resilience, and encouragement for others who face this journey."

—DIANE C. POMERANTZ, PH.D., Clinical Psychologist, author, *Lost in the Reflecting Pool: A Memoir*

DEFYING THE VERDICT

MY BIPOLAR LIFE

CHARITA COLE BROWN

CURBSIDE SPLENDOR
Chicago Independent Publishing

CURBSIDE SPLENDOR PUBLISHING

Published by Curbside Splendor Publishing, Inc., Chicago, Illinois in 2018.

First Edition
Copyright © 2018 by Charita Cole Brown
Library of Congress Control Number: 2018932087
ISBN 9781945883071

Edited by Josh Bohnsack
Cover and interior design by Alban Fischer

Manufactured in the United States of America.

curbsidesplendor.com

AUTHOR'S NOTE

I relied on my memories to create *Defying the Verdict: My Bipolar Life*. Therefore, it is a subjective recollection: My truth.

Although this is a work of nonfiction, I have changed the names of some people and places to protect the privacy of specific loved ones.

To my family of origin: Leonard and Anita Cole,
Valerie Cole-James, Karen Cole Wouldridge,
Kelvin Cole, Ernestine Cole Nelson,
Linda Cole Little, and Martin Cole.

To my cousin, Theodora Stanley (1949-2015)
for praying that I would one day
share what I did to get well.

DEFYING THE VERDICT

CHAPTER ONE

"Stare the rat down."

—JAMES BALDWIN

SPRINGFIELD HOSPITAL CENTER
HISTORY SHEET

D: 3-15-82

R: 3-16-82

T: 3-16-82

NAME COLE, Charita Lynette   CASE NO. 103278

MARCH 15, 1982

This 22-year-old, black, female, college student is admitted on A-Certificates from Sinai Hospital because "She is excited, manicky, hallucinating auditorily from God, paranoid, grandiose and delusional, unpredictable, somewhat violent and out of control".

She is brought in on stretcher, quite agitated, uncooperative to interview saying, "where is my husband?" and refuses to answer. When questioned again to get more information says, "fuck you", then very agitated and unmanageable. So, she is taken directly to ward and seclusion room. She is well developed, well nourished and physically not in distress. Denies alcohol and drug abuse. Her memory, intelligence, orientation and abstraction capacity cannot be assessed. She has no insight, totally impaired judgement and excited and agitated mood and unpredictable behavior. She is quite angry and hostile.

PROVISIONAL DIAGNOSES:

Axis I: 296.40 Bipolar disorder, manic type
          295.70 Schizoaffective Disorder,
                 excited type
          295.20 Schizophrenia, catatonic,
                 excited

Axis II: 799.90 Diagnosis deferred on Axis II

Axis III: Deferred

ADMIT: Hitchman A-Wing

MKK:cab   Myun-Ki Kim, M.D.

M-234   INTAKE - RECEPTION NOTE

SPRINGFIELD HOSPITAL CENTER
HISTORY SHEET

D:3-16-82
R:3-17-82
T:3-17-82

NAME <u>COLE, Charita Lynette</u> CASE NO. <u>103278</u>

MARCH 16, 1982

This 22-year-old, black, female patient was admitted to this hospital for the first time on March 15, 1982 with two doctors certificates signed at Sinai Hospital beacause she was excited, manicky, hallucinating auditorily, hearing voices from God, paranoid with grandiose delusional ideation, unpredictability and some violent behavior.

On admission here she was quite uncooperative to the interviewer saying where is her husband and refusing to answer any questions and when she was further questioned she said, "fuck you" and in a very agitated manner. She was immediately taken to the ward and placed in the seclusion room.

In this interview the patient was quite out of contact with reality and not wanting to cooperate with the interviewing situation, so, I obtained the following information from her mother.

The patient was born in Baltimore City and was raised by her parents. Her mother is 50-years-old and a Teacher. Her father is also 50-years-old, a Chemical Operator. They seem to be getting along well. She has four sisters, the oldest one is 26, married with no children. She is a Senior Accountant Executive in a bank. She has another sister who is 24 and living with her aunt because she is single and she works as a Correctional Officer. She has another sister who is 18, a student at Coppin State College and a 15-year-old sister who is a student in high school. According to the mother, the patient's mother's mother, the grandmother, was in Springfield Hospital and Crownsville Hospital several times. The patent's mother's uncle was seen by a psychiatrist and the patient's father's sister was mentally retarded and died. The patient's mother was seen in psychiatric outpatient at Phipps Clinic and she has not been on any medicine since 1973. There was nobody in the family who committed suicide.

The patient attends Wesleyan College in Connecticut and she was in her fourth year, a very good student, majoring in English.

The patient was never married. She has had no recent boy friends but in the past she was observed to have a boy friend by her mother. She has been hospitalized once in December, 1980 and January, 1981 at Connecticut Valley State Hospital in Middletown, Connecticut for two weeks, Diagnosed as Hypomanic. Since then, she has had no outpatient therapy except a few times she was seen at Sinai Outpatient Clinic and was not given any medication. The patient is reported to have no medical problems. According to the mother, the patient is not drinking and does not abuse Marijuana and takes no other drugs. According to the mother, the patient is in Apostolic Religion since 1979 converting from Catholic and according to this religion, is not allowed to abuse those drugs. She has never been arrested.

I. Turek, M.D.:cab

I PSYCHIATRIC HISTORY

CHAPTER TWO

"Are we all captive to the scars of our family history,
no matter what we do?"
—JOHN BLAKE (CNN)

WHEN I WAS seven years old, my maternal grandmother, Ruth Stanley Ross, came to live with my family, the Coles, in Baltimore, Maryland. She joined my parents, my five siblings: Valerie, Karen, Kelvin, Ernestine, Linda and me plus our dog Rover in our two story row house.

I can still see Granny Ruth, a caramel-colored black lady in her fifties who stood five feet, three inches tall. She always wore a housecoat, socks and slides or slippers in the house. When going out, she wore stockings tied just above the knee with matronly slip-on shoes. She never wore makeup. Her eyes sparkled. She had a ready smile and an irreverent sense of humor, speaking things in my hearing that my devout, sober-minded Catholic mother would have prohibited, deeming such utterances inappropriate for young ears. My favorite was, "If you're sad, stick two fingers up your tail and get glad." Of course I didn't know the connotation of this phrase. The idea of anyone doing that seemed outlandishly funny to me. I welcomed the occasional bawdiness. Granny's zest for life amused and delighted me.

Granny quickly became a welcomed member of our working class Baltimore neighborhood. It was the late 1960s, a time when people were neighborly, sharing flour, sugar, eggs and ketchup. My mom shared these things and loaned encyclopedias as well. As the neighborhood's elementary school teacher in residence, she promoted education and willingly lent from her stockpile of books which included the Harvard Classics.

Our corner house had one of the largest yards—plus, a non-working barbecue pit in its corner—plenty of space to play and make mud pies. Since my outgoing grandmother spent much of her time at home with our family, she quickly became a part of the neighborhood. The children in the neighborhood grew to know and love her. Many of them called her Granny right along with "the Cole clan," as Mama referred to us.

Granny's residency at our house on Finney Avenue ended abruptly on a spring day in 1969. After I arrived home from school, before I could change out of my school uniform, I noticed my grandmother had propped our front door open with a porch chair. This was unusual. Granny always lectured, "Keep that door closed so bugs won't fly in this house," What happened next was even stranger.

Wild eyed, my grandmother began hefting our living room furniture onto the porch. Out went a lamp. Out went an end table. Out went a chair...She performed her task frantically, with unusual strength, like an erratic Hercules.

My three-year-old sister, Linda, who was usually right up under my grandmother, was staring at Granny from the couch that remained in the living room, tears forming in her eyes.

Though she spoke to herself under her breath, I think I heard my mother say, "I have to do this." Trembling a little, she picked up the phone's receiver and dialed. I scrambled over to the sofa to grab my baby sister. She was crying, silently.

Mama pleaded into the phone for help before placing it back on the hook. Standing transfixed on the far side of the living room, she could see the street outside our front window, while keeping an eye on my sister and me. She avoided Granny until the police arrived, in what seemed like less than a minute.

My mother walked out to the porch and stood behind Granny as two officers walked up our front steps. They spoke calmly to my grandmother. "Ma'am, exactly what's happening here? What's going on?"

From inside the house, I heard Granny scream, "Go away and leave me alone."

I ran to the window and saw one of the officers take my grandmother by the arm. She yelled, "Get away from me," then turned and punched him in the chest.

In response to this unexpected resistance, the policemen handcuffed my usually docile grandmother, cited her with disturbing the peace and placed her in the police car. Not long after they arrived, they drove away. By this time, my older sisters were standing inside the front door with our mother. She was shaken, not tearful.

Grabbing my little sister by the hand, we walked upstairs to my parents' room. She began to cry audibly. I sat on the bed and held her on my lap. Five-year-old, Teenie, lay next to us in wide-eyed silence.

At the time, I couldn't understand why Mama didn't ask the officers to calm Granny down without taking her away.

Years later, Mama explained that she had been forced to call for police assistance on an earlier occasion, when we lived in an apartment on Lakewood Avenue in 1961. Having grown up with an actively bipolar mother, she was acutely aware of the times when her mother's behavior escalated beyond her control.

After this incident, I did not trust police officers, despite Officer Friendly's yearly visits to my elementary school classrooms.

That night, after the pieces of furniture had been returned to their respective places and every child had been sent to bed, I listened through my parents' closed bedroom door as my father comforted my mother in hushed tones. No one attempted to quell the fear I felt in response to Granny being forcibly removed from our home. For me, it seemed like "out of sight, out of mind." Worse yet...I had no idea where the police had taken her. About two weeks later, I got my answer.

It was a lovely Sunday afternoon. My father announced that

our family would be visiting our grandmother. We drove for about an hour. When we got to the grounds there was a sign that read, "Springfield State Hospital." *When had Granny gotten sick?* I wondered. I looked around at the grounds. *At least she's in a beautiful place*, I thought. After entering the building, I was jarred by the buzzer that sounded as we entered the door of the locked ward. We were entering a Maryland state psychiatric hospital, a holding center for the mentally insane. Looking back, I was so overwhelmed by the experience that I do not remember whether or not my four younger siblings, including my new baby brother were with us. I do remember my parents and my two older sisters being there. My parents acted like this was an ordinary Sunday visit.

Because this was an asylum for blacks without financial means, the walls were cheerless and the room had a slight pungency—not clean, like I expected a hospital to be. Some of the patients moved stiffly, like zombies, while others moved erratically, like wind-up toys at the end of a rotation. I didn't know I was witnessing the effects of heavy sedation, medication or even electroshock therapy in the zombies—these were the primary psychiatric remedies of that time. I guess the wind-up group needed their medication adjusted.

As the attendant led an older female zombie to the area where my family was seated, I asked myself, *Who is this lifeless old lady? And why are they bringing her over to join my family?* Then I realized: This was my beloved Granny. *Where was the sparkle in her eyes?*

My parents talked. My sisters smiled and sat nicely. Normally the most loquacious of the Cole sisters, I had nothing to say. After hugging Granny, I sat silently, longing to go home. The hour-long visit seemed unending. We left the ward accompanied by the sound of that buzzer and the clanging of the door closing behind us. We had to leave my grandmother at Springfield. We got back in the car and my father drove home. Though my mother had been pretty quiet on our way to the hospital, she conversed with my sisters a little on the way home. As for me, I sat silently between my sisters, my thoughts in overdrive. My nine-year-old mind began to process my Springfield visit. I concluded that people who walked around like zombies or behaved erratically were definitely *crazy*. This conclusion unnerved me even more than Granny's departure in handcuffs had.

The Springfield visit spawned a taproot of fear within me. The roots spread as time passed. As an adult, I still wish my parents had spared me that seemingly benign visit to the psychiatric facility. But how could they have known they should have left me at home? In their minds we had simply visited a hospital. In mine, overly sensitive Charita Cole had just stared at her worst fear.

This was the last time I would see my grandmother.

After her release from Springfield, Granny chose to live in Baltimore city with a woman who had been her caregiver, rather than return to Finney Avenue. One afternoon, while at home alone, she attempted to light the gas oven with a match. Apparently, after turning the gas on, she waited too long to touch the match to the stove. Fire exploded from the oven, igniting her housecoat. In shock, she ran from the kitchen, through the living room and outside onto the sidewalk. A passing driver saw her. He pulled his car over quickly and smothered the flames with a blanket he had in his car. My grandmother was hospitalized with second and third degree burns over at least seventy-five percent of her body. She passed away the following day. Because her face wasn't burned, her body rested in a half opened blue casket. She wore a flowy blue shroud and held rosary beads between her gloved fingers. Our family and many of our neighbors profoundly mourned the death of Ruth Hester Stanley Ross. She was sixty years old.

As I GREW older, I sometimes experienced disturbing and disjointed thoughts that increased in frequency with the passage of time. In eighth grade, fearing the worst, I decided to share my suspicion about myself with my oldest sister. Though she was only four years older, I trusted her wisdom. "Val," I whispered, "I think I might be crazy." She answered, matter-of-factly, "Charita, everybody's crazy."

CHAPTER THREE

"There are children who are told they are too sensitive, and there are people who believe sensitivity is a problem that can be fixed in the way that crooked teeth can be fixed and made straight."

—LYNDA BARRY

I DON'T REMEMBER specific incidents in my life before age four. I recall a general sense of happiness and security when in my parents' presence. As a college student, I remember being saddened when I met people who felt unloved. I would declare, "As long as my mother's living, I know somebody loves me." Her love was a nearly tangible thread that connected the two of us. After all, I spent my pre-school years attached to her apron-strings.

As for my father . . . he played prominently in my earliest memory. I was four years old the night I woke from sleep riding in the backseat of a station wagon. As I got my bearings, I saw my dad in the front passenger seat. His closest childhood friend, Willie, steered the car as we travelled from Baltimore, Maryland, where we lived, to Chapel Hill, North Carolina, where they were raised. I was a little perturbed when I noticed my two year old brother, Kelvin, lying next to me in the very back of the wagon. This was in the early 1960s before seat belts or car seats were a legal requirement for children under five. I forgave my dad for bringing him. I decided to enjoy spending time with my dad without my sisters.

As it turned out, Daddy and Uncle Willie were going to visit their respective mothers and, unbeknownst to me, my father was planning to leave me in Chapel Hill with his parents. I became suspicious when my dad pulled out a suitcase full of my clothes. My brother's weekend wardrobe was in my dad's suitcase. My grandparents wanted me to spend some time with them. Granny Lillian informed me that my older sisters would join us when they got out of school for the summer in two months.

Honestly, I had too many attachment issues to stay by myself in North Carolina with grandparents I barely knew. My four-year-old self decided I was not going to be separated from Daddy, period. I had a tearful meltdown.

When Uncle Willie drove back to Baltimore a couple of days later, my suitcase and I were in that car with Daddy and Kelvin. I returned to my grandparents' house two months later to spend the summer, accompanied by my sisters, Valerie and Karen. I felt safe with them.

My mother insists my childhood hysterics often disarmed my dad, even lessening the severity of consequences for my wrongdoings. When I became an adult, she insisted, "Nobody wanted to hear all that noise."

Always a crybaby, my parents labelled me 'high strung' for my sometimes extreme levels of excitability and nervousness. Several years ago, my dad revealed that his mother made sure he was aware of how high strung my mom was, before he married her. Granny Lillian did not want him to go into marriage unadvisedly, as the vows say. So my temperament was neither new nor surprising to him. As a child, one parent or the other sometimes instructed me to rest my nerves—to go someplace alone to read a book, to listen to music, or to simply sit and relax.

I wish I could say I saved my emotionalism for my parents. But that wasn't so. I was the little girl who cried every day in my morning Kindergarten class. I never felt comfortable with the other children nor with Mrs. Black, the stranger who I called teacher. I didn't understand why I had to go to school. Why couldn't I just stay at home with my mother?

One day, tired of the crying, Mrs. Black exhaled sharply, and covered my mouth with her hand. I bit her palm. I waited nervously for my mom to pick me up at the end of the morning. I knew I was in for a spanking, but my teacher didn't report what I had done in response to what she had done. However, that reaction to my continual weeping did shape me up a little. I stopped crying for about two weeks. It was a win-win for both of us. I never got punished for blatant disrespect and she got a brief reprieve from my emotionalism.

In first grade, I cried all the way to school for months. The tears annoyed my sisters, the second and fourth graders who walked alongside me everyday, but what could they do? I was their sister. My mother always taught her children that we had to support one another. She frequently told us, "You are all you have." Having been an only child, she demanded solidarity within our sibling group.

When winter came, one neighbor, who greeted me from her porch most mornings, would smile and caution me that my tears might freeze on my face. I kept crying. My embarrassed older sisters wished they could let five-year-old Charita walk the five blocks to school alone.

Once I got to school, I was basically fine until things didn't go my way. My sister still talks about the day she was summoned from her second grade classroom to make me stop crying. My teacher would not give me an eraser to remove an errant mark from my paper. First graders used fat pencils without erasers. Karen found the whole scenario ridiculous. At seven years old, what was she supposed to do to quiet her younger sister? Of course, she couldn't tell my teacher that. Children were never allowed to challenge a nun's decisions.

But everything about first grade wasn't negative. That was the year I learned an important Biblical truth. Sister Robert Marie taught us that God is everywhere. Talk about an epiphany! When I got home from school that day, I ran into every room. I looked under beds and in closets, proclaiming, "God is here!" I always knew God lived in our beautiful Catholic Church with the stained glass windows and the pipe organ. That was on Sundays. But now I learned God was with me everywhere every day.

Before this grand religious epiphany, my knowledge of God was based on my encounters with Him at Sunday Mass at St. Ambrose Roman Catholic Church. Although we prayed to God at home, I had always believed He lived in this stately stone building with its dark stained glass windows and a bell that chimed from the bellows of the church, welcoming me. Once inside, I dipped my hand in the holy water at the door of the sanctuary and genuflected, before entering the pew with my mom and my siblings. My dad only came to church for special occasions like baptisms or First Communions.

The stations-of-the-cross adorned the walls to remind me of Christ's crucifixion. As a child, I never really understood why we kept Jesus hanging up on the big cross at the front of the sanctuary. The nuns taught us Jesus was alive. I just accepted the crucifix as a necessary part of our ritual. When I was very young, the mass was conducted in Latin. This mysterious language added to my sense of wonder. We sat, knelt and stood at the same predetermined segments of each service. Mass was almost magical for me, especially when the priest waved the incense and its heady odor filled the sanctuary. The musical strains from the pipe organ in the balcony seemed to descend directly from heaven.

The most mystical occurrence took place near the end of the Mass. Each Sunday the priest performed a ritual that turned ordinary wafers into the body of Christ. Any person who had received First Holy Communion could come forth and receive Christ on the inside. I longed for the opportunity to participate in this sacred ritual. Many years later, as a third grader, I finally got my wish.

First Communion was usually the highlight of second grade, but our class had to wait an additional year for the sacrament. Sister William Mary thought, as a group, we lacked the necessary maturity to take such an important doctrinal step. By that time, the Mass was conducted in English and I had a better understanding of what was going on during the service. My one sad discovery was that the organ music was not coming directly from heaven.

Third grade was also the year Karen placed a lighted candle in the kitchen window. She turned to me and asked, "Wouldn't this look pretty at Christmas?" Whoosh! The curtains caught fire. If not for Granny Ruth's quick action, extinguishing the flame with a tea towel, the curtains might not have been the only thing destroyed in the kitchen.

When my dad got home from work, Karen swore we were both responsible for the fire. I tearfully recounted what had really happened, but my dad spanked us both. "We could have been left with no place to live!" he shouted. Later that night, when we were alone, Karen admitted she lied about my involvement in the curtain incident. She was getting me back for the last whipping she had gotten. We had been scuffling on a bed in our room, when I heard my dad on the stairs. I immediately stopped punching, began screaming, and lay under her, helplessly. We were breaking a Cole family sibling rule—*No physical fighting with one another*. Although Granny insisted, "Karen and Charita were both fighting," Daddy chose to believe his eyes instead of his ears. My dad only spanked Karen, erroneously believing I was her victim.

By fourth grade, I stopped crying. Now I had a new problem: academic boredom. Noting this, my teacher, Ann Jacobs, created some stimulating activities for me. I remember creating a science bulletin board about mollusks. She also took me to the Baltimore Museum of Art, my first trip to a museum. That trip ignited my love for museums. In December, at Miss Jacob's suggestion, I was chosen to narrate the school's Christmas program.

As if being a great teacher who provided enriching activities was not enough, Miss Jacobs found a new school for me to attend,

The Park School of Baltimore, Inc., an independent school located in Brooklandville, Maryland, just outside of Baltimore City. One of her friends, Mr. Russell, taught high school English there. Certain the curriculum would challenge me, she walked my mother and me through the application process. I was accepted, but my mom was told that the scholarship money she would need to cover my tuition was only available to students entering seventh grade and above.

The admissions letter stated I would be an asset to the class of 1977. My mother was encouraged to have me re-apply in sixth grade for seventh grade admission. Mama, Miss Jacobs and I were disappointed. Miss Jacobs took my mom and me out to lunch to celebrate anyway. The positive takeaway for me: at lunch they explained an asset was someone who adds value, not a female donkey.

I almost didn't make it to fifth grade. One late summer evening in 1969, Karen and I went outside to roll up the car windows before nightfall. We raced out our back door, ran across the lawn and scrambled over the fence to the car parked near the far corner of the house. A faster runner, she usually reached the car first and rolled up the driver's side windows, leaving the passenger side for me.

However, this evening Karen slipped on the grass, and I reached the driver's side first. That meant I got to sit behind the steering wheel. As we cranked up the windows, I decided we needed some excitement. My sister would have been content to follow our normal routine of locking up the car and going back inside. Not me. Shutting the driver's side door while seated in the driver's seat, I turned to Karen and suggested, "Let's play policemen." Karen replied, "Charita, stop playing and get out of the car." Then with her older sister authority, she added, "It's time to go back in the house."

By this time, Karen's feet were on the curb. I had no plans to get out with her. I was going to play policemen by myself, if necessary. Placing one hand on the steering wheel and the other on the gearshift, I put the car in neutral. When the car began to shift, I was surprised. I hadn't considered the fact that the car was parked on a downward incline. As the car moved forward, so did my sister: from the car seat to the pavement. She got in the house quickly, having jumped over the fence in one leap, before running into the house for help. The passenger door slammed shut as it hit the tree alongside the house. I believed I was facing death as the car started to roll toward the stone wall at the foot of the hill.

As the car slowly gained momentum, I climbed from the front seat to the back seat then returned to the front seat in a continuous motion. Now immobilized by fear, I wasn't sure what to do next. If my father's car hit that wall my tail would be grass. As the car headed across the intersection at the far corner of my house, my neighbor, Mr. Cook, saw a child at the wheel of my dad's car. Powered by adrenaline, he ran beside the car, shouting, "Roll the window down." When the window was down far enough, he reached inside the car, grabbed the wheel and steered the car up the grassy hill midway between the corner and the wall. The car came to a complete stop. Mr. Cook helped me out of the car, placed his arm around me and asked, "Are you all right?" Before I could answer, I looked up and saw my mother rushing toward me. Scooping me into her arms, she thanked our neighbor for saving me. After examining me for possible physical injury, she said, "My husband was asleep. He's on his way. If it's okay with you, I'm going to take Charita back up the street." Mr. Cook agreed to wait by the car for my dad while Mama took me home. She put her arm around me, supporting my weight as she led me back up the hill, up our front steps and into the house. By the time we reached the porch, my breathing pattern had almost become a wheeze. I had to prepare for my meeting with my father.

After my mother assured him I would be okay, my father went down the street to thank Mr. Cook. He would also try to piece together exactly what happened. Less importantly, he would check the condition of the car. I was surprised as I figured out that Karen had not related exactly how the car slipped out of gear. Although my attention seeking behavior irked her, she kept my transgression a secret. I discovered we had an actual sister code.While my dad talked to Mr. Cook and returned the car to the side of our house in the same condition it had been earlier, my mother prepared a pallet for me on the living room floor with a blanket and a pillow. She thought lying still on the cool hardwood floor might improve my breathing. As I lay there, I clearly understood I had almost destroyed my father's car and maybe myself along with it. By the time Daddy re-entered the house, I appeared very weak, wheezing more heartily than before. It was just enough to earn my dad's compassion rather than corporal punishment.

In sixth grade, I began taking what I now label mental health days. Every third week, my dad's swing shift as a laborer at a local chemical company, required he work from seven in the morning to three in the afternoon. Sometimes, during these weeks, I would take one day off from school during which I would stay home and rest my nerves. Or I would stay home with a stiff neck, a somatic condition that was eased by lying down with a hot water bottle wrapped in a towel placed against my neck. No adult ever chided me about my absences. Maybe because my grades remained stellar . . . That year, my parents and I reapplied for admission to The Park School.

I was accepted and awarded a six year full tuition scholarship.

CHAPTER FOUR

"Change, when it comes, cracks everything open."

—DOROTHY ALLISON

THE SEPTEMBER AFTER Granny Ruth died, I enrolled at the prestigious Park School on a full tuition scholarship. My St. Ambrose classmates and my fellow parishioners lauded my achievement, and I believe the timing of my school change unduly boosted my mother's pride in me. She began to show me undeserved preferential treatment. I had siblings who were just as smart as me. Smarter even.

My brother Kelvin, two years my junior, barely spoke before age three. Then, at age four, he taught himself to read . . . the newspaper. I learned to read in first grade, like most children of that time.

I still remember sitting in the living room chair, studying my green vocabulary card. My brother would stand behind me as I read the words aloud. When I stumbled over a word, Kelvin would pronounce it correctly, audibly. "Mama," I bellowed, "he's doing it again. Makes him stop." Then came my mother's reply from the kitchen. "Kelvin, leave your sister alone." He'd walk away, for five or ten minutes.

And, as Karen dutifully reminded me through the years, I was "sucking up the family's resources at that school." I agreed. The money my mother spent for incidentals, like lunches purchased from the school cafeteria, gym uniforms and books, should have been spent on my siblings instead. My excitement over attending Park was tempered by guilt and a feeling that I would be beholden to my family forever, like an indentured servant whose debt would never be repaid.

St. Ambrose School educated black and white working class, mostly Catholic students. My first day in seventh grade, I discovered I was the only black girl in the class. My new school educated an affluent, largely Jewish population. I felt like a foreign exchange oddity.

To keep me from "smelling myself," as Granny Ruth would say, my mother would remind me of my station, saying things like, "You might go to that school, but you're still a poor little black girl." The comments not only bruised my spirit, but also confused me. Up to this point in my life, I considered myself to be like every other person. No better. No worse. Her comments heightened my awareness of the disconnect between my working class home culture and my upper middle class school culture. Then I noticed, all the black adults at school worked in the cafeteria or on the janitorial staff. In my mind, it seemed they were the schools lower stratum, the subservient class.

One day, in math class, a boy mocked my incorrect pronunciation of fourth. I had pronounced it "fourf." I laughed along with some of my classmates. Laughter became my defense mechanism at school. Though the teacher reprimanded him, my confidence took a hit. After that incident, I sometimes withheld correct answers, fearing I might pronounce something wrong and be the object of another cruel joke. Though unaware of its genesis, my eighth grade science teacher corrected this reticence. He told me, "I won't know what you're thinking if you don't speak up. It's okay to give a wrong answer. I can only help you correct incorrect answers I hear." Because of this comment, I recommitted to my right to be heard. One of my seventh grade teachers had already warned us against pairing diarrhea of the mouth with constipation of the mind. I would still avoid those maladies.

By the end of seventh grade, I had become close to my classmate, Denise, another first year Park student. I was no stranger to wooded areas, but she was a nature expert, able to name more types of trees than oaks, elms, and pines. During our free periods, we would cross over a wooden bridge into the woods on the school grounds. On these excursions, we'd walk along the trails, talking and singing. On warm days, we would take our shoes and socks off and walk in the stream. She taught me how to find its spring in order to drink cool, clean water without having to go back inside. As much as I enjoyed my friendship with Denise, the Park School was an alien culture I was ready to escape.

By eighth grade, my home life was becoming increasingly unpleasant. I was still highly sensitive. The atmosphere in our overcrowded row home overwhelmed me. Sometimes, I would go into the basement, sit atop the washing machine, and read, sing, or cry. I needed to rest my nerves.

Unlike in my early years, my parents never seemed to get along. In 1968, Daddy wanted to move our family to Delaware where his job was being relocated. Mama, pregnant with my youngest sibling, nixed the idea of uprooting the family. We stayed in Baltimore. Daddy got a new job, but this seemed to place a wedge in their relationship.

Mama tried to get me—and all of her children, for that matter—to align with her against Daddy, making disparaging marks to us about him. I attempted to get along with both parents. I often ended up in the crossfire of their disagreements. I eventually became the mediator child, trying to keep peace between parental factions, while also serving as go-between for my parents and my siblings. On more than one occasion, when I agreed with my father on a point of contention, my mother snarled, "That's right, Charita. You're the wife. You understand him."

Yuck, I would think. For me this statement had unnatural overtones. I was too young to understand my mom was simply venting anger over her marital situation. Personalizing her comments, I found it necessary to try harder to make her know I wasn't a complete defector.

Mama related how she met my father at a birthday party for one of her students. The party was at the child's house, where

Daddy was a boarder. After serving in the Korean War, he and Uncle Willie had relocated to Baltimore from Chapel Hill, NC, hoping to improve their circumstances. According to my mother, "Leonard seemed like a gentleman. He worked every day and seemed like he cared for his mother." They married in 1957.

Daddy was usually open to answering any of my questions One day, alone in the kitchen with him, I asked, gently, "Why don't you and Mama just get a divorce?" *Why did I ask that?* His answer exploded from his mouth. Had I been a cartoon character rather than a living eighth grader, the force of the response would have caused me to complete a backward roll. I was shocked by the intensity of his reply. I don't remember exactly what he said.

Apparently, my parents shared a love I didn't understand. Nor did I want to. I now understand that my father took the vows "to have and to hold from this day forward, for better, for worse," seriously. It didn't matter that I would have labelled their relationship, *worser*, if that had been a word.

This incident taught me not to meddle in grown folks business. For the rest of my childhood, I never discussed any opinion I might have held about my parents' ending their marriage. At least, not with either of them. After this interaction, I added fear to the love and respect I held for my dad.

In September of eighth grade, during my physical, the school doctor asked, "How are you enjoying The Park School?" At Park, most adults asked students questions, expecting thoughtful answers. My response revealed my general unhappiness, while remaining true to my father's credo, "What goes on in this house, stays in this house." I told her about being in a different section than my friend, without mentioning any personal family business. My real feelings about my life were summed up in the Jackson 5 song, "Corner of the Sky." I sang it often from my perch on our washing machine.

Cats fit on the windowsill.
Children fit in the snow.
Why do I feel I don't fit in anywhere I go?
Gotta find my corner of the sky.

The doctor shared our conversation with my eighth grade English teacher, Richard Peyton. A Park School graduate himself, he believed in making The Park School a racially and socioeconomically diverse, progressive learning environment. He encouraged me to remain at Park. Throughout the year, he suggested specific ways for me to make school and life more enjoyable. Initially, he offered to have me reassigned to the same eighth grade section as Denise, my stream walking friend. Making that change would have removed me from his class, so I declined. Per his suggestion, each of my older sisters shadowed with me for a day at Park to become more familiar with the school culture. I had shared my guilt about attending Park while my siblings went to public schools. We hoped, after a school visit, they, Karen especially, would acknowledge Park was a better fit for me than their citywide magnet school would be.

Valerie enjoyed her visit. She ended up shadowing a friend of hers from Western High who was now a student at Park. Karen had a great day, but retained her belief that I should go to public school.

Noting my love of reading, Mr. Peyton taught me to search for meaningful solutions to life's problems in books. I also learned to connect themes between texts. These lessons became life-affirming habits.

Once a week, I read to second grade students during their library period. I'm sure I had opportunities to share Russell Hoban's books about Frances the Badger with them. Frances had spunk, like me. She even made up songs to correspond to life's struggles, like I did. Francis' wise mother loved her unequivocally, always making decisions that were best for her. I now understand my Mama also made decisions that were best for me.

In our final conversation about where I would attend high school, I attempted to convince my mother I could receive a great education at Western High, the public magnet school Valerie and Karen attended. I never mentioned craving Karen's friendship and approval. Mama told me, simply, "You don't understand the opportunity you've been given."

In September 1973, I entered ninth grade at The Park School.

CHAPTER FIVE

"Champion the right to be yourself. Dare to be different and set your own pattern; live your own life and follow your own star."

—LIN YUTANG

Sometimes situations unexpectedly work in my favor.

My newly hired ninth grade English teacher, Jeannette Davis, was an African-American woman. Having a black teacher made me feel a little less odd. In the Park School tradition, she helped students hone critical thinking skills. We read works from authors of color, including Chinua Achebe and Lorraine Hansberry. Being exposed to works by non-white authors, one student complained, "I feel like this is turning into a black studies course." Jeannette acknowledged his displeasure, and continued exposing us to literature new to the Park School curriculum.

Lorraine Hansberry taught me important life lessons through her play, *A Raisin in the Sun*. The Younger family seemed more like actual people than fictional characters. I identified with Beneatha Younger. She reflected the energy, stubbornness and even self-absorption I displayed with my family. Carefully attending to Beneatha's epiphanies as a gifted, young, black woman, I internalized the importance of persistence and being non-judgmental. She held fast to her dream of becoming a doctor, despite the financial challenge she faced after her older brother, Walter, lost the money reserved for her medical school tuition in an unauthorized liquor store venture. After a tirade in which she labeled her brother worthless, her mother reproved her. "When you starts measuring somebody, measure him right, child, measure him right. Make sure you done taken into account what hills and valleys he come through before he got wherever he is."

However, the book that impacted me most that year was Sylvia Plath's novel, *The Bell Jar*. Esther Greenwood was a brilliant Smith College student whose life was disrupted by manic depression, now known as bipolar disorder. She underwent shock therapy after an unsuccessful suicide attempt. By this time, I was quite adept at personalizing literature. Esther and I shared a similar sensibility. In the back of my mind, I believed what happened to her, could happen to me.

Jeanette told us the book was a fictionalized account of Plath's experience. We read her poetry along with the novel. A few years later, I performed Plath's "Mad Girl's Love Song," as a spoken word poem. I was horrified to learn she committed suicide in her early thirties. After turning on the gas oven in her London flat, she placed her head inside, asphyxiating herself.

The nuns had already convinced me suicide was the unpardonable sin. They intoned, "If you kill yourself you cannot go to heaven. You will not go to purgatory. God does not forgive people who've killed themselves. People who kill themselves are consigned to hell." I doubted I would ever commit suicide because I WAS DETERMINED TO AVOID SPENDING AN ETERNITY IN HELL.

Besides critically reading novels, plays and poetry, our ninth grade curriculum included an advertising unit. We studied ways in which specific words are employed to drive consumerism and influence belief systems. I created a personal slogan, *I am different and unique.* I repeated this internal mantra, attempting to convince myself not fitting in was just fine. When my peers would say, in the vernacular of the day, "Charita, you're a trip," my casual response became, "I'm not a trip, I'm a journey." I gave myself permission to live within my own parameters.

At Park, each high school student selected an advisor. I chose Jeannette. In a one on one conversation, I shared my assessment of the financial burden I placed on my parents by attending Park. She gently informed me, "Whether or not your parents can afford to send you to a private school is their decision as parents. As a child, it is your job to learn all you can while you are here. Whether or not they can afford to send you here is not your concern." After our meeting, she called my mom and had a long conversation with her about the things I had shared.

That Saturday, Mama, my sister Valerie, and I sat down in our living room to talk about my feelings. Although I no longer spoke so quickly when agitated that I had to "suck back spit to keep from drooling," in the words of my cousin, Lela, I still exhibited quite a range of emotion. Histrionically, I confessed to my mom, "I know you can't afford to send me to Park." For emphasis, I added "I feel poor when I'm at school." That comment launched a conversation that forced my mother to examine her role in developing my poverty mindset. She stopped asserting I was a poor little black girl. As always, Valerie encouraged me, "You should be proud that you're smart enough to get a scholarship to go to private school."

That afternoon, I lay down to rest my nerves without anyone suggesting I do so.

I returned to school on Monday, feeling a little calmer. I reconciled myself to the fact I wouldn't be leaving Park.

To encourage me, Jeanette gave me a ticket to a matinee performance of The Alvin Ailey American Dance Theater, an African-American modern dance company at the Lyric Theater in Baltimore. It was the first time I had seen a live, professional dance performance. Watching The Nutcracker on television didn't count. I sat spellbound throughout the performance. This artistically excellent group of black dancers impressed me. A decade or so before, companies like this did not exist. I was so inspired that I took modern dance classes, beginning in tenth grade.

Jeanette left Park at the beginning of my tenth grade year. She was a godsend, another teacher who bolstered my flagging self-esteem. She and Marian Dixon, an African-American woman from my church encouraged me during my early high school years.

Marian Dixon was one of my mother's teacher friends. She

attended St. Ambrose Church and was a founding member of Baltimoreans United in Leadership Development (BUILD.) BUILD is a not-for-profit, interfaith, multiracial organization created to make the city of Baltimore more livable. The organization promoted change within people, and Mrs. Dixon supported change within me.

When I shared how difficult it was for me to study in my bustling household she created a study space for me in her home down the street from mine. She took me along when running errands and taught me how to sew. Respecting my intellect, she engaged me in meaningful discussions. Spending time with her underscored my value. By listening to me, Mrs. Dixon taught me that my opinions were worth listening to.

CHAPTER SIX

"Life is a process of becoming, either becoming more or becoming less. I'm becoming more by a process of choosing what I become."

—LLOYD STEPHENSON

By tenth grade, St. Ambrose Roman Catholic Church had morphed into a predominantly African-American congregation. After a few years of folk masses, which I loved, we had now moved on to a Sunday Mass featuring contemporary gospel music. Our Caucasian priests were still the norm, and each of our two African-American deacons had a wife, according to the Catholic Church's new ordinance. The nuns assigned to our parish no longer wore traditional habits, though they sometimes wore veils. My mom's friend, Sister Cecelia, declared they often came in handy. "I got out of receiving a ticket when the police officer came up to the car and realized I was a nun."

I worked as an evening receptionist at the rectory several times per week in eleventh and twelfth grades. I also prepared breakfast every other Sunday morning. Being around the clergy gave me an opportunity to know and respect the people who served the congregation. To me, these were trustworthy, regular people with positive motives who had accepted a call to serve God in a different capacity than the laity. One of our priests, Father Henry Zerhusen, especially exemplified Christ-like compassion. He treated each congregant like someone who mattered. That kindness drew people to the congregation. Harvey was one of the people that kindness drew in.

Harvey, a high school student who was a few years older than I, was one of the unchurched neighborhood kids Father Henry ministered to. He spent as much time as he could at the rectory. Professing a love for God, Harvey aspired to become St. Ambrose parish's first African-American priest. Though Harvey was well-regarded by many parishioners, I thought that if he ever became a priest, he'd be more like the evil cleric Rasputin than any priest I've ever seen at St. Ambrose..

Harvey never seemed to like me very much. Because he was

a student at the zoned high school, I felt he was jealous of my private school education. I also believed he resented the fact that the members of my family, one of the families that integrated the church in the early 1960s, failed to regard him with awe. However, many long-time St. Ambrose parishioners delighted in his evangelical spirit. To his credit, several classmates he brought to church converted to Catholicism. This was a pretty good evangelism record for someone who had been Catholic fewer than five years.

One fall evening, Harvey joined me in the office where I sat at the secretary's desk answering the phone. I half-listened as he rambled on using big words—some correctly, some incorrectly—until I heard him say, pejoratively, "Your mother is crazy." That got my attention. Forget about sticks and stones or even hearing what he said, in context. I sprang from my chair and kneed him in the groin, exclaiming, "My mother is not crazy!" He had officially pressed my button. No one was allowed to associate the word crazy with my mother, a woman who once soldiered through a significant bout of depression.

This was not the first time I became angry when I suspected someone was calling Mama crazy.

In sixth grade, Sister Marie Carl informed our class, "Only crazy people talk to themselves." Having heard my mother reason aloud from time to time, I raised my hand. When she called on me, I corrected her. "That's not true," I declared. She refuted my statement. Then, for the first time, I yelled disrespectfully at a nun. "My mother talks to herself sometimes and my mother is not crazy." That outburst earned me a trip to the principal's office with Sr. Carl's hurriedly handwritten note in hand.

Because I was one of the good kids, who had just made her school look good by earning a scholarship offer to a prestigious private school, the principal listened thoughtfully to my side of the story. Once I calmed myself down, she firmly, then gently informed me my "flippant behavior would not be tolerated." I apologized to my teacher.

By the time I calmed myself down in the Harvey incident, he had left the office. I went home and tried to call him at the rectory the next day. I failed to reach him. Being the kind of Christian he was, when I left the rectory the following night, he had a female friend follow me home with a small posse while he remained at the rectory. When they caught up to me, Harvey's ally announced, "You hit my friend, now I'm going to hit you." She punched me in the mouth, gave me a menacing stare and went back in the direction she came, accompanied by her followers.

I did not hit her back. She terrified me. She had recently been released from a juvenile detention facility for girls. And truthfully, I felt I got what I deserved. In the eye-for-an-eye world, my action had been inexcusable. I called and apologized to the duplicitous Harvey after the attack. The next day at school, when people asked how my lip had gotten swollen, I lied, "I tripped in my house and hit my mouth on the corner of a dresser."

The following year, I had to decide whether or not I was ready to commit myself to the Catholic faith. I chose to be confirmed. Once the bishop anointed my head, I would be "sealed with the Holy Spirit." When he asked if I was ready to serve the Lord with my whole being, I gave the prescribed answer, "I am ready and willing," with vigor. I wanted to be a better person.

That spring, one of the young adults at St. Ambrose decided our parish would participate in the Catholic Youth Organization one-act play competition for the Baltimore diocese. We would be the only non-Caucasian participants. Our director chose the work of a local playwright, Faith Walker, entitled, *The Everlasting Arm*. I auditioned, reading Beneatha's monologue from *A Raisin in the Sun*.

The play is about an elderly woman—my character—and her three children, the youngest of them having passed away. I was always thankful that Gregory was cast as the younger brother. One evening, Karen came to watch me rehearse. She pulled her lighter out of her purse and flicked it against the cigarette she had placed between her lips. The flame setting had become higher as the lighter was thrown in her bag, and it ignited the front of her perfectly shaped Afro. While I stood frozen, Gregory immediately used his script to extinguish the flames. That was how my father discovered Karen was a smoker. It was also one of the few times he held back his retribution against her. With second-degree burns on her forehead, she had suffered enough. She wore a realistic looking wig until her hair grew back. It took years for the scars on her forehead to heal. Thanks to Gregory, one of Harvey's converts, I still had my sister.

Our play moved from the semi-finals to the finals, where we placed second. My fourth grade teacher's friend, Mr. Russell, still taught at Park and was one of the judges. On Monday, as part of the morning announcements, the assistant principal announced, "We'd like to congratulate Charita Cole. She was awarded the best actress trophy in the Catholic Youth Organization's one-act play competition on Saturday." Before that day, I intentionally separated my home life from my school life. The two intersected now.

That summer, upon invitation, I participated in Park's six-week Summer Arts Program, studying drama, at no cost. This would be the first of two summers in the program. The second summer, the director found a way for me to be a paid participant through a special grant opportunity for inner-city high school students.

In September 1975, my eleventh grade year, Lloyd Stephenson arrived at St Ambrose Rectory. An African-American college senior at St. Mary's Seminary in Baltimore, he elected to live at St. Ambrose throughout that year, to the betterment of our parish.

Lloyd stood six feet, five inches tall and studied ballet. He introduced our congregation to liturgical dance, performing self-choreographed pieces in traditional attire. He produced and directed a Good Friday passion play in which he portrayed Jesus. I was surprised when the people my brother Kelvin called "the old heads" participated willingly. Our new seminarian challenged them to expand their religious borders.

He launched a teen youth group for high school students—to expand our cultural borders. Some members of the group, including me, attended plays in theaters for the first time. At our weekly Sunday-evening meetings usually held in Lloyd's separate parlor, we engaged in informal discussions of life and faith. One of our meetings centered on how each of us envisioned the Trinity. *It's about time someone actively encouraged us to think about and articulate what we believe,* I thought, with Park School exuberance.

I was drawn to Lloyd's keen intellect, exceptional confidence and maturity. Although he saw the same Harvey I did, he treated him respectfully. Harvey resented the young people's acceptance of a new spiritual mentor. Lloyd challenged the HNIC—Head Negro In Charge—status he had created in his own mind. To me, Harvey's ego seemed a little deflated by the success this unwanted intruder was having with the parishioners. I was glad Harvey was unhappy. As Mama would say, there was no love lost between Harvey and me.

Karen, Lloyd, and I sometimes went to movies or out to eat without the rest of the group. Spending time with us, he encouraged us to become our best selves. His internal confidence bolstered mine. Not caring what others thought of him, he would tell me, "I know I'm a wonderful person." Winking at me, his close friend, he would add, "So are you." I loved spending time with a person so sure of himself, and of me.

Lloyd graduated in May 1976, returning to his hometown of Roanoke, Virginia for the summer before completing his studies for the priesthood in Rome. I still have postcards and a scarf he bought me while studying in Europe. Our communication became more sporadic as time passed.

Lloyd and I reconnected in the mid 1990s. I was in Newport News, Virginia visiting a friend who lived near his assigned parish. She invited him to her home for home-baked lasagna. As we caught up on one another's lives, I shared my bipolar diagnosis and thanked him for setting an example of unapologetic fearlessness for me. Shortly thereafter, Lloyd and I lost touch.

When I started writing this memoir, I googled Lloyd's name to find his address. I wanted to share my project with him, being certain he would offer inspiring words of encouragement. As a graduate of the Pontifical North American College in Rome, his information wouldn't be hard to find. I found his obituary. Reverend Lloyd Franklin Stephenson had died in March 2004 at age forty-nine.

I printed out the obituary and wept, saddened by my loss as well as my inability to pay my final respects. Thankfully, Lloyd knew I appreciated the lessons he taught me about being emotionally honest with myself.

CHAPTER SEVEN

"It is the mark of an educated mind to be able to entertain a thought without accepting it."

—ARISTOTLE

SENIOR YEAR WAS filled with activity.

The summer before senior year, I met Jerry. I had boyfriends before him, but this was my first relationship. We were introduced by a mutual friend. When we met, he told me he had first noticed me at St. Ambrose. He and his older sister usually sat on the side of the church where I served as an usher. I was impressed by this smart and attractive college sophomore who appreciated my intellect.

We shared the classic first love where you stay on the phone at night until one or the other of you falls asleep. I was usually the sleepyhead. Jerry provided emotional support for me and encouraged my love of theater. He was my first thought and only love for many years. My father and Lloyd do not count.

Loving performance, I was delighted to be cast in the school's fall drama, Bertolt Brecht's *Caucasian Chalk Circle*. The director, Rosemary Knower, a first-year faculty member, had held auditions for Federico Garcia Lorca's *Blood Wedding*. I noted the play had been changed when my friend, Bernice, and I saw the posted cast list. Bernice joined my class at Park in ninth grade, boosting the number of black girls in the class of 1977 to two. Having bonded over time, we rushed to the school library to find a copy of the play and see what size my part was.

To my delight, my character, Grusha Vashnadze, a young Russian peasant woman, was the lead. During the rehearsal process, Mrs. Knower, the director would sometimes take me home for dinner with her family so I would have a ride back to school for evening rehearsals. One night at dinner, she shared how difficult she had thought Brecht's plays would be for high school students to perform. She said to me, "Your audition changed my mind." Coming from Mrs. Knower, an artistically insightful director, I was thrilled. *Maybe with time, the acting thing could work out for me.*

The play was well received. My entire immediate family attended the Saturday night performance, including Aunt Nellie and Uncle Vernon, my surrogate grandparents on my mom's side of the family. Jerry came to every performance. He and I skipped the cast party to celebrate my performance alone.

I experienced something unusual, for me anyway, in mid-October of 1976. In my whirl of activity—rehearsals, applications, college visits, and home-life—I felt exhausted. Then came the crying.

I had stopped crying in school in third grade after several instances in which Sister Frances Ann had sarcastically instructed one of my classmates to "get a bucket from the coatroom, and hold it near her to collect her tears." The nuns never seemed to understand the negative effects of public shaming on children's psyches.

I was sitting alone in a classroom during my blue period when a fellow senior entered the room. Seeing tears on the face of one of her fellow upbeat classmates, she attempted to cheer me up. In tenth grade, one of our American history classmates had dubbed her, "the little bubble that never bursts." She reminded me of my academic prowess, asserting with positivity, "Everything is going to be alright, and as smart as you are, you'll definitely get into a great college." As seniors, we were focused on finding and being admitted to the school that best fit. I regained emotional control.

A few days later, I began to cry uncontrollably again, for no apparent reason. Bernice led me from the library to the classroom of my advisor, Kenneth Greif, during his free period. He agreed with her suggestion that she drive me home. I went to bed and slept so many hours I missed school the next day.

I needed somewhere more quiet than my house to rest the nerves that seemed to be unraveling. At my request, I spent the following week with my Aunt Nellie and Uncle Vernon. They were like grandparents to the Cole siblings. Aunt Nellie, my grandmother's sister, raised Mama when Granny Ruth became too ill to care for her. Their peaceful home was nearby, and I could get to school easily from their house.

Within the next few weeks, I was back to my normally energetic self, reenergized, like a toy with a fresh battery. After that episode, one of the girls in the *Caucasian Chalk Circle* cast told me, based on my inertia, "I thought you might have been dying."

Though encountering my first bout of severe depression, I was still responsible for completing my college applications. One day, in order to make sure I completed my National Achievement Finalist application on time, Mr. Greif had me sequester myself in a classroom. I forced myself to focus and plod through the essay which resulted in my eligibility to receive scholarship money.

Depression never frightened me. I saw it as something one could recover from.

My mother had suffered a bout of depression when I was around twelve. I had accompanied her to the Phipps Clinic, the outpatient psychiatric clinic at The Johns Hopkins Hospital. I sat in the waiting room while she consulted with the doctor. The psychiatrist advised her to take a leave of absence from teaching to get some much-needed rest. She also took medication, as directed. Regaining normal functioning after a month or so, she returned to work without overemphasizing this blue period.

Despite being a devout, rule-following Catholic, she gave birth to seven children of varying temperaments. I often wondered if having fewer of us would have better suited her Type A temperament. I wasn't aware of how being raised by an actively bipolar mother may have scarred her emotionally. As it was, she loved us and trained each of us to know and love God.

One year, when asked what she wanted for Christmas, she replied without hesitation, "peace of mind." On December 25th, my youngest brother and sister presented our mother with a box wrapped in shiny paper, with a gift tag reading, "To Mommy. Love, Linda and Martin." She opened her present and pulled back the tissue, revealing a piece of lined paper, on which they had written in bold, capital letters: *PEACE OF MIND.*

My mother's daughter, peace was what I craved to bookend the unconditional love my family provided me.

CHAPTER EIGHT

"Appreciate your learning process, for it is of equal value to realize there is need for change as for the change itself."

—BETH JOHNSON

IT WAS A Sunday night in mid-May, shortly after eleven. Jerry was bringing me home after spending time with Karen in her freshman dorm at the University of Maryland, Baltimore County. As we rounded the corner at the top of my street, we saw a fire truck—parked in front of my house. Unable to get any closer, Jerry parked the car up the street from my house. Getting out of the car, we could smell the smoke. With my stomach knotted and my heart beating erratically, I raced toward the truck. I saw firefighters, but none of my family.

Turning to Jerry, I shrieked, "Oh God, No! Where is my family?" the first thought that bombarded my mind.

Before I could reach a firefighter, an elderly neighbor took me by the arm and informed me my family was okay. Mama and my siblings were at Mrs. Dixon's house. My father was on his way home from work.

Jerry and I went down the street to Mrs. Dixon's. Seeing us coming, Mrs. Dixon opened the door, let us in the house and hugged me. After we were inside, my youngest, soot-covered sister, Linda, described what happened. Bernice and I awarded her the unofficial melodrama of the year prize for her description.

"I woke up and everything was black. Everybody was asleep. I smelled smoke. I yelled for Mommy and woke up Teenie, I could barely see through the black smoke, but I felt my way into Kelvin and Martin's room, screaming for them to wake up. Then we walked down the stairs quickly, like in a fire drill, and out onto the porch. It was terrible." She concluded, "Mrs. Dixon had us come down here to her house while we waited for the firefighters to arrive."

That's when I noticed all of my siblings were wearing night clothes. My mom had on a robe. Thank God everyone made it out. In hindsight, Linda's description doesn't seem so melodramatic at all.

The fire department determined the blaze was caused by an electrical short in the kitchen. The next day we were able to enter the house and retrieve our clothes. The fire had been contained to the main floor of the house. We lost our childhood pictures and I lost my Best Actress trophy.

Our family was split up into different living environments. My parents and brothers stayed with one of my dad's friends who lived around the corner from us. Valerie remained in her apartment at University of Maryland, College Park. Linda lived with friends of the family. Teenie and I lived with Aunt Nellie, as did Karen during her school breaks. I remember feeling a little displaced, being separated from most of my family. However, I never felt homeless because I lived with Aunt Nellie, our family's matriarch.

During a round of college applications and campus visits in the fall of 1976, I visited Wesleyan University, in Middletown, Connecticut. I fell in love with the library. It housed an impressive number of books. Entering the stacks, I knew I could be quite at home here. In eleventh and twelfth grades, when inundated with work, I would go to the Central Branch of Enoch Pratt Free Library to study in its hallowed hush.

I had applied at Mr. Greif's suggestion. Knowing me well, he believed Wesleyan would provide an optimal learning environment for me. I added it to the list of colleges I had prepared with my college guidance counselor. Before acceptances arrived, I had considered matriculating at Williams College with Bernice, but I was wait-listed.

Having accepted Wesleyan's admissions offer and the National Achievement Scholarship awarded to me, I looked forward to the comfort of borrowing books from and studying in the Olin Library.

AT SCHOOL, WE ended our senior year with a personally designed, self-directed senior project. I taught first grade reading at St. Ambrose and completed the course, Child Care and Development in the Kindergarten at Park. I also continued dance lessons.

Each senior was required to orally synopsize his or her project for eleventh graders and members of the upper school faculty. I described my six-week program, tying it into lessons learned at Park. My presentation included a dance solo I choreographed, assisted by my beloved dance teacher, Martita Goshen. I began studying modern and jazz dance with her in tenth grade. I discovered dance was the only activity that silenced the tickertape parade of thoughts that generally bombarded my brain. I selected the Negro spiritual, "Hush! Somebody's Calling My Name" as featured in the Alex Haley drama, *Roots*, for my performance. I was honored when Mr. Lakin, my exacting American history instructor, called it, "the best presentation I've seen this year."

A rainy day had forced graduation inside. The people with whom I shared the closest bond were there. I had received extra tickets—enough for my large immediate family as well as Aunt Nellie, Uncle Vernon and Jerry.

Sitting on the familiar theater stage as part of the Park School graduating class of 1977, I half-listened to the selected commencement speakers. Not attending to what they were saying, I thought about what lay behind me as well as what loomed ahead. When diplomas were presented, I accepted mine proudly.

By the end of my senior year, after completing an extensive, reflective senior questionnaire about my Park School experience, I acknowledged to my mother, "You were right. In eighth grade, I didn't understand or appreciate the quality of a Park School education. I doubt I would have developed the critical thinking skills at Western that I absorbed at Park."

My learned ability to reason, question assumptions, and think things through in order to formulate reasonable, appropriate plans of action would be essential for future decision making. It was the system I would need to help me override my abundant feelings and eventually manage my unpredictable moods. I was in great physical, mental, and emotional health. Graduating from Park was like bursting out of a womb—with very high Apgar scores.

CHAPTER NINE

"We ask ourselves, who am I to be brilliant, gorgeous, talented,
fabulous? Actually, who are you not to be?
You are a child of God."
—MARIANNE WILLIAMSON

IN JANUARY OF my senior year, I was introduced to improvisational theater. Cora, a classmate from school and fellow summer
arts participant, had auditioned for an improvisational theater
group forming at Baltimore's Theatre Project. The auditions were
open to high school juniors and seniors. When I called the theater
at lunchtime from the pay phone at school, I was informed the
auditions were over. They were finalizing the participation roster.
After calling back every day for a week, I was invited to audition
for the ensemble.

At fifteen, while performing in *The Everlasting Arm*, I learned
to transfer my emotions to characters in scripted drama. Now, I
learned improvisation technique alongside students from other
Baltimore-area high schools. We explored creative theater techniques, developing the awareness of our bodies in space that is
necessary when interacting with others spontaneously.

I learned that improvisation requires control. We practiced
establishing eye contact to predict one another's movements. I
excelled at holding my body completely still for tableaus, and I
could spin in a circle longer than anyone else in the group thanks
to learning *spotting* for dance, a technique where you have the
same distinct focal point for each turn.

During the improvisation workshop, we were encouraged to
pinpoint our strengths. I identified storytelling as an area of personal gifting. In our final workshop session, when participants
took turns exaggerating one another's strengths, I remember one
of the guys in the group taking center stage to imitate me telling
a story, using a high-pitched voice. I have since learned to control
my pitch.

The Theatre Project's director, Philip Arnoult, created the
theater venue in 1971 to make improvisational theater by performers from the United States and other countries available to

theatergoers in Baltimore. Inspired by the success of our teen improv group, he created a program using us as core performers. His concept became the Baltimore Neighborhood Arts Circus. Professional avant-garde artists partnered with members of our group as well as additional students hired and trained for this summer arts endeavor. Our mission was simply to bring theater to Baltimore's clearly defined neighborhoods. With a grant from the Baltimore Arts Council, we performed Tuesday through Saturday for eight weeks during the summer of 1977. The neighborhood launch followed a prep week with our individual teams during which time we honed such skills as mime, juggling, storytelling, and performance chants before the neighborhood launch.

Because we were off on Monday, my friend Debbie and I renamed that day Circus Sunday, and planned activities together. Our friendship was meaningful, charged with spontaneity as well as complementarity. We spent hours talking about our lives, sharing thoughts with each other that we had never shared with anyone else. We were able to share our deeper feelings with one another, creating a grounded relationship.

Throughout the inaugural Circus Summer, in a spirit of community, we chanted, played games, sang songs, juggled and taught neighbors to do so as well. Each week, teams traveled to different neighborhood parks and recreation centers to set up our metaphorical tents. Students were paid through the city. We were given complimentary metro bus passes to travel around the city without personal cost. Because my family had been living apart since the housefire, I sometimes brought Linda along. It was my way of maintaining my connection with my baby sister.

Gomo, an African drummer, often travelled with my group. I wanted to play percussion along with another young woman. Denying me that privilege, he smiled and affirmed, "You're a dancer, baby." Dancing was indeed what I needed to do to keep my head clear.

Meeting people from different neighborhoods and traveling around the city independently increased my self-confidence and my readiness to go off to college alone and leave my beloved Baltimore behind. Not to mention the fact that I would be separated from my parents and siblings for the first extended period.

4536 Finney Avenue may have been psychically uncomfortable for me at times, but it was home—the place, in the words of Robert Frost, where "when you have to go there, they have to take you in."

The more difficult separation I endured before college was the end of my relationship with my boyfriend, Jerry. He, along with Bernice, anchored me successfully through the depression of 1976. Although we continued to go out throughout the summer, he officially ended our relationship just before my graduation. He explained, "I don't think you can sustain a long-distance relationship." When I visited Williams College that January, I had come back raving about a young male student I met who I thought would make a great friend. At the time, I did not understand how he could have seen that as a potential problem. Besides, I was matriculating at Wesleyan, not Williams.

The real beginning of the end was my reaction to the poem Jerry wrote me in April, which ended, *"The young will play, the old will rest / The stars will shine brightly in the sky / And I will always love you, or at least try."* When I laughed inappropriately as his reading ended, unsure of how to respond to this sentiment, he ripped the paper up. Though I gathered the pieces and kept them, I bruised his ego. I wish I could attribute this to an illness rather than my emotional immaturity.

Though devastated, I suppressed the impact of having my heart put through a meat grinder before being placed back in my chest.

I accepted Jerry's decision and in the spirit of improvisation, I concluded, *I loved like a seventeen year old. I suppose that love just wasn't strong enough.* Shutting off the love valve, I continued, *After all, I'm going away to concentrate on getting an education.* Being dumped was difficult for me. I repressed the rejection I felt confronting the loss of my first love.With nothing constraining me, I could uproot myself from Baltimore and replant myself in whatever place I fancied.

CHAPTER TEN

"somebody / anybody /
sing a black girl's song"
—NTOZAKE SHANGE

I PACKED THE last of my belongings the morning of my departure for Wesleyan. I had spent time with my parents, Linda, and my brothers the day before. Karen and Teenie were at the house saying goodbye as Uncle Vernon helped place my two large suitcases and my trunk into the rear of his station wagon. Having stayed up late partying with friends the previous night, I was bleary-eyed as he drove me to Baltimore's Pennsylvania Station.

After helping me check my belongings, Uncle Vernon waited with me in the train station until it was time to board the train. Though tired, I felt a slight adrenaline rush as I settled into my seat on the railcar. In six hours, I would arrive at Meriden station, the closest station to Middletown. A Wesleyan student was scheduled to meet me upon arrival and drive me to campus. I looked out the window, wishing Baltimore a silent farewell before falling asleep.

I was briefly awakened when the conductor in New York asked me to show my ticket again for the last half of the trip. The next thing I knew, he was calling through the railcar, "Meriden is next. Meriden station will be our next station stop." I went to the restroom and splashed my eyes. I was beginning a brand new life.

Upon arrival, my volunteer driver and I loaded my things into her car, chatting about the school during the twenty-minute trip. We arrived on campus at the Malcolm X house, the African-American specialty house in which I would share a two-room double with my roommate, Michelle. When I arrived, she had claimed the inner, more private room. The outer room was mine. Michelle was a pre-med student from Brooklyn. After we became friends, she called me her *artsy-fartsy* roommate from Baltimore.

That evening, Michelle and I went to dinner in the dining hall where most of the black students were sitting together on the right side of the cafeteria. We joined them. I was excited to see so many black faces at school. Though in reality, the black population was ten percent of the total populace of my senior class at Park. The ice cream and freshly baked bread were especially delicious, definite contributors to the freshman fifteen.

After dinner, I convinced Michelle to walk with me around campus using the maps we had been given in our welcome packets. As a member of the Baltimore Neighborhood Arts Circus, I had grown accustomed to quickly familiarizing myself with new territory. And I didn't want to seem lost, but that spoke to control issues, not fear of new places.

I entered Wesleyan planning to pursue a dual major in psychology and theater. Thinking psychology would be an academic fit for me, I enrolled in Foundations of Contemporary Psychology. The course proved more difficult to get through than I expected, when I staggered into depression at the end of the semester.

However, I learned and embraced an applicable psychological truth, Abraham Maslow's theory of self-actualization. Maslow depicted human needs being met according to a hierarchical pyramid. He listed physiological needs at the lowest level, followed by the need for safety in body and resources. The middle level, at which many people get stuck, was the need for love and belonging, followed by the self-confidence and respect tier. The pinnacle of the pyramid was self-actualization, where a person perfects herself in the areas of creativity, problem-solving, and lack of prejudice. I saw myself living between levels four and five. As I studied psychology, I believed I would ascend to level five and eventually become a therapeutic helper.

Participants in Introduction to Acting were required to audition. I chose a monologue from Angelina Weld Grimke's play *Rachel* as my audition piece. The judging panel of three theater professors included Esteban Vega, a person of color, whose production choices brought multiracial theatrical opportunities to Wesleyan students. Esteban was impressed by my choice from the work of a female playwright who was part of the Harlem Renaissance.

The auditions unearthed so much talent that the panel decided to offer two sections of the course instead of the customary single section. I went to the bookstore to buy my books before the class lists were posted. Seeing the bookstore only stocked enough books for one section, I grabbed the Stanislavsky methods book and placed it in my basket. A classmate who had also auditioned for the class was present at the time. "You're buying the book?" he questioned. "We don't even know if we're in the class."

"You might not know, but I'll be chosen for the class," I responded confidently. Unlike me, my classmate had to wait for the second shipment of books to get his copy.

In October, Esteban planned a trip to Broadway through Ujamaa, the black student union. We saw the matinee performance of Vinette Carrol's *Your Arms Too Short to Box with God* followed by an evening performance of Ntozake Shange's *for colored girls who have considered suicide/when the rainbow is enuf*. The first play excited me, being the first Broadway show I had ever seen. The second play amazed me, resonating in my spirit, as the actresses taught me the reality of what women can become when they bind together. At the end of this choreopoem, the women repeat, "I found god in myself & I loved her fiercely." They embraced the rainbow, the promise of success, rejecting suicidal impulses.

The play was a great companion piece to the female empowerment album I had listened to repeatedly the previous summer, *Nightbirds* by Labelle, featuring the songs "All Girl Band" and "Lady Marmalade." Having bought a copy of the play *for colored girls*, I performed one of the monologues, "Toussaint," as my final project for Introduction to Acting. As my life continued, reading poems from *for colored girls* became an essential routine for me.

Besides our resident advisor, everyone who lived on the upper level of the Malcolm X house that year was a young woman. We developed a comradery over the course of the semester. I became especially close with my roommate Michelle as well as Leslie, a female freshman who lived in the Butterfield dorms. Early in the semester, using the list of African American students in the class of 1981 provided by my RA, and in Arts Circus style, I searched out and connected with each of my fellow minority freshmen.

To provide an opportunity for us to know each other, I planned the black freshman party at the Malcolm X house, providing grain alcohol-spiked punch for the attendees. Only seventeen, I enlisted a senior to purchase the alcohol for me. Not a lover of alcohol, I only tasted my concoction; the sweetness of the juice masked the potency of the liquor.

During mid-semester break, I visited Bernice at Williams College. I had planned to catch a bus back to Wesleyan. While there, I ran into the Dean from my school who gave me a ride back to campus. One of Wesleyan's first African-American graduates, he was interested in how I was enjoying my first semester and inquired about my future plans. I shared my love of theater and my wish to become a children's psychologist with him. The Dean bought into my enthusiastic confidence.

In November, I was an extra in the play adaptation of Richard Wright's *Native Son*, directed by Esteban. I also assisted the costumer for the play, *The Lion in Winter*. Students in Introduction to Acting were required to participate in one performance-related activity outside of class. I chose two activities because my mood had heightened. Although my energy level was up, my productivity level decreased.

As my thoughts and behavior began to escalate, I started forgetting things. I left a costume I had repaired for the lead actress in *The Lion in Winter* in a friend's room. Because she had gone out of town, I used heightened sensual charm to convince her resident advisor to let me in to retrieve it. I fell behind in attendance at compulsory language lab sessions for my French class and eventually dropped the course.

I got a ride home for Thanksgiving with a hall mate who was spending the holiday in Washington, DC. While at home, I overheard Mama mention my father had developed arthritis in his spine. Processing her words in my emotionally heightened state, I assumed the condition was severe. Irrational thoughts of my father being sick and maybe even dying triggered the strongest melancholy I had ever experienced.

When I returned to campus, I was awash with sadness. I cried often, but I forced myself to memorize my monologue and study for my psychology final. Lacking the energy to complete my final English paper, I arranged an extension with my instructor.

I didn't want any of my peers to know, but I set up an appointment with the school psychologist. Although it was not my viewpoint, I knew many black people shunned psychotherapy. I slunk from the Malcolm X house to the student behavioral health center located directly behind it.

Philippa Coughlin, Ph.D., founded and directed the Office of Behavioral Health for Students at Wesleyan University beginning in the early 1970s. She was an early pioneer in the field of behavioral health for college students. She worked with Carl Rogers at the University of Wisconsin-Madison, earning a doctorate in humanistic psychology. Rejecting psychoanalysis, Rogers taught people how to thrive in an environment of genuineness, acceptance, and empathy. Dr. Rogers believed people self-actualize when their ideal selves and their self-images match. Dr. Coughlin's therapeutic style was informed by this point of view.

After three sessions with Dr. Coughlin, in which I shared my depression from senior year, we decided I would benefit from a medical leave of absence. I would see a therapist in Baltimore and schedule an appointment with her in September for reinstatement.

I stored some of my belongings at Malcolm X, taking mostly clothing home with me. I assured the friends who expressed concern over my extreme sadness that I would be okay, and they would see me in September. As I boarded the train, I believed my mood would improve and that I would return to Wesleyan for the following fall semester.

Treating this semester as a false start, I rehearsed to myself, *being a colored girl, I will move on to the end of my rainbow.*

CHAPTER ELEVEN

"Get Up! You are not defeated!"

—CAMRYN D. LITTLE

I RETURNED TO White Oak Avenue, experiencing what my future college roommate Penny and I later labelled *the brink of abysmal despair*. I spoke to a couple of friends from Park the week after I came home, attempting to process what went wrong my first semester at Wesleyan.

After Christmas, I spent mornings in bed, enveloped in a cocoon of self-pity. But my Aunt Nellie was not going to allow me to succumb to defeat. On an early January evening, my aunt came home from work to find me fully clothed, lying on the bed, staring at the ceiling, eyes filled with tears. When she sat on the other bed in the room, I hoped she was about to sign off on my self-sabotage. After all, I was the one who had to take a semester off from school, shaming myself by lacking the inner strength to move forward.

Contrary to my expectation, Aunt Nellie began telling me that I was able to pull myself together. She used herself as an example. At that time, though she and Uncle Vernon had separated, she refused to let the separation, which later ended, derail her life. As she said, "Charita, when you're feeling bad for yourself, you have to realize there is always someone else worse off than you." She shared how she continued to be pleasant at work and how, when she found it too emotionally painful to worship at the same church as my uncle, she went to another church. She continued, "No matter how bad you think your life has become, there's always something to be grateful for. You have to decide what that is."

I was able to receive Aunt Nellie's wise counsel. I was fortunate to be staying with her during this trying time. After that talk, I thought about how right my aunt was. I went to Loyola University and received counsel from Father Geary, a Jesuit priest whom Father Henry referred me to. One of the nuns at St. Ambrose suggested that my depression was "anger turned inward," but Father

Geary and I did not think I was angry. We met weekly for a couple of months until my mood had normalized.

Feeling better, I began looking for employment and preparing family meals. Soon after I returned from school, my cousin and her two sons moved back home. Of course, I was used to living with many people, and I enjoyed my younger cousins.

I owed my English instructor a final paper, which I completed at my aunt's house and mailed to him. He sent me a note, remarking how well-written the paper was, better than my other endeavors that semester. Something about the stillness of being with my family allowed me to write at the level I had written while at Park.

At my urging, Karen, Lela, and I saw the touring company of *for colored girls who have considered suicide* in Baltimore in February. The play was a booster shot for me. The rainbow was still enough.

In March, I got a job at a Rite Aid drugstore as a cashier. I reconnected with Debbie who was rehearsing for her role as Dorothy in the musical, *The Wiz*, at her high school. A petite actress with a terrific voice, she wowed the audience. The guys who played the tin man, the scarecrow, and the cowardly lion were equally talented. This was a lovely theatrical diversion in my time away from Wesleyan.

I also reconnected with Cora from Park School and the improv group. She was waiting to hear from Julliard, where she later matriculated to study theater. Besides academic excellence, she displayed acting ability that exceeded that of most of our contemporaries. In the years to come, when Cora became a professional television actress, Karen would sometimes question, "Why are you wasting your talent in that church when you could be an actress like Cora?"

That summer, I returned to The Baltimore Neighborhood Arts Circus for a second year. This time I was co-leader of the team called Summer Fun. We had a theme song and specialized in children's theater. Frank, who played the scarecrow in *The Wiz*, was a member of my team. We developed a close friendship through which I tried, unsuccessfully, to cozy up to his best friend, Cedric.

Years later, as Linda and I reminisced about that Circus summer, I asked, "Why do you think Cedric didn't want to be in a relationship with me?"

Linda looked at me quizzically. "What would he have looked like being interested in you when his best friend loved you?" Until my sister made that comment, I had no idea Frank was interested in me. Because he never brought it up, I considered us good friends who spent lots of time together.

We moved back into our home on Finney Avenue in July of 1978. In preparation, my dad bought the necessary furniture. Being removed from our home for a year psychologically depleted my mother. It seemed she lacked the energy to prepare our house for the family's reentry. Valerie and I stepped up, picking out curtains, trash cans, dishes, and linens.

Years later, when I tried to get Mama to talk about how she felt during the year we were displaced from our home, she informed me, in her characteristically succinct manner, "living outside of her home was an unpleasant experience."

Looking at this situation from my mother's perspective, I would guess being forced to spend time away from her children would be difficult, bordering on traumatic. Having been raised by a bipolar mother who abandoned her more than once while manic, she would never have chosen to be separated from any of her minor children.

CHAPTER TWELVE

"A faithful friend is a sturdy shelter:
he that has found one has found a treasure."

—BOOK OF WISDOM 6:14

AT SUMMER'S END, feeling both calm and confident, I returned to Connecticut for round two of college life. At the end of our forty-five minute session, Dr. Coughlin determined I was mentally healthy enough to resume a full-time course schedule.

Gloria Penny Mullings, a sophomore, welcomed me as her new roommate. She lived in a large double in a William Street high rise. Ordinarily, upperclassmen lived there, but because her roommate had decided to take a year off, she could choose whom she wanted to live with her. Since the apartment had a full kitchen, I wouldn't need to pay for a meal plan.

I believe we are often drawn to people who are similar to those we are accustomed to. Penny reminded me of my sister, Karen, who never suffered fools lightly and judged situations as black or white. I process in technicolor. We were like Kansas and Oz. By the end of the semester, we had become friends. I sometimes accompanied her to her home in New Haven, an hour south of Middletown, when she went to visit her mother. Her father had passed away from lung cancer during her sophomore year; therefore, she chose to be present for her mom as they grieved.

In October, my mother visited for four days to make sure my reintegration at school was smooth. She met my friends and made dinner for groups of us. She especially loved my friend Veda's new baby, Marian. I had the pleasure of helping Veda care for her daughter as she completed senior year.

Cheryl, a freshman from Philadelphia, became another close friend that year. She taught me how to speak ubby-dubby, a fictional language created for the PBS children's program, *Zoom*. My freshman year, a friend informed me I was "like one of those *Zoom* kids." Cheryl explained the *Zoom* kid uber-excited vibe to me. In ubby-dubby, my name was Chubbarubbitubba, hers was Chubberubbyl.

Cheryl noted my unique conversational style. I jumped from subject to subject in a non-linear way. I would go from A to D to B back to A and on to C before returning to A. She was the first person to point out to me that most people didn't speak this way. Although some "normal" people speak this way, it can be a bipolar marker, as it was for me.

Esteban directed Steve Carter's play *Eden* that semester and sent the stage manager to suggest I audition. I declined, having decided to concentrate on academics that semester. As it turns out, I should have auditioned. Penny had a role in the play. As much time as I spent running lines with her and attending rehearsals and performances, I was almost part of the cast anyway.

My favorite course that semester was Afro-American Narrative, taught by Professor Robert O'Meally, a brilliant African-American academic, who had written the definitive biography of *Invisible Man* author, Ralph Ellison as his doctoral thesis.

Professor O'Meally introduced me to the writings of Zora Neale Hurston, an African-American female anthropologist and novelist who was part of the Harlem Renaissance. I was excited to discover a female counterpart of Langston Hughes and Countee Cullen. As a black female writer, I considered Hurston one of my literary heroes.

That semester, Iju, a gorgeous, young African man in the class of 1981 captivated my attention. Insisting I was not his type, my girlfriends made comments like "Your hair is not long enough, nor is your skin light enough for his tastes." What did they know? Fully confident that I could entice him, I made sure he knew of my interest in him. I was flirtatious, without being too forward.

In February, I saw a sign on the student post office bulletin board declaring February as "Go For It" month. Whatever you wanted, you should go after it, full throttle. So I decided to invite

Iju to be my date for the Sadie Hawkins dance, a dance for which women were supposed to invite dates of their choosing. He accepted my invitation, but not my advances. I am convinced that had he entered into a relationship with me, I would have lost my budding interest in growing closer to God. I would have chosen a man I could see and touch over the invisible God. Therefore, I'm glad no relationship flourished between us.

In the spring semester of 1979, I was cast as Clytemnestra in a student-directed production of *The Oresteia* by Aeschylus. The play was the culmination of an ungraded course called Aeschylus, Our Contemporary, taught and directed by a senior theater major as part of his honors thesis. I was delighted to be cast in a classical Greek tragedy. The ensemble performance was performed on the University's main stage. Valerie and Karen came to Wesleyan by train for the performance. Iju came as well, to my surprise and delight. I had been mindful to send him a formal invitation. Although he never told me he was present, I noticed him in the audience.

Robert Fagles, whose translation of the play we used as our script, attended the Friday night performance and the reception immediately following. He came over to me and engaged me in conversation about my performance, which he considered brilliant. As Mr. Fagles moved on to talk with the play's director, Jon Esteban Vega, who had been in earshot, encouraged me to get the translator's feedback in writing for my portfolio. I failed to follow his advice. However, Robert Fagles's feedback underscored my belief that I was a legitimate actor.

That year, I befriended another student who shared his backstory of battling depression in high school. His successful battle with mental illness convinced me I could live in a healthy emotional space. To ensure depression would not envelop me, I willed myself to stop crying. I decided that the crying symbolized weakness and true colored girls don't cry.

Throughout the years I struggled through mental health crises, I could always rely on Penny's support. Many years later, noting that she'd never known anyone with bipolar disorder before she met me, I asked, "Why did you continue to support me in all my craziness?"

She answered, "Because we're friends."

To which I say, *"Ain't it good to know you've got a friend."*

CHAPTER THIRTEEN

"All is calm. All is bright."

—"SILENT NIGHT"

VEDA GRADUATED IN May and moved back to Arkansas with her daughter, Marian. After graduation, I spent a week in Philadelphia with Cheryl. When we went to the zoo, one of the animals inspired a title for the children's book I vowed to write, *The Great Escape of the Barbary Ape*. That creature looked so miserable in that cage. He seemed to understand he was boxed in.

We went to the theater to view French foreign language films. Indulging our inner children, we read from Michael Bond's *Paddington*. We spent time with Cheryl's older sister whose self-confidence inspired me. On the final night of my stay, Cheryl's mom took us to an Atlantic City casino. It was my first and only casino trip. I won $25.00 playing the slot machines. Not a gambler, I pocketed my winnings.

Then I returned to Baltimore for Kelvin's graduation. Her mom had passed away in April. I persuaded Penny to join my family for the weekend. In an attempt to cheer herself up, she referred to herself as *Orpheline*, the French word for orphan. My family offered emotional support. My cousin Lela adopted her as a little sister. Karen's date got us tickets to see a Patti LaBelle concert. Patti's incomparable performance seemed to brighten her spirits a little.

After Kelvin's graduation, I went to Chapel Hill, North Carolina to spend time with Granny Lillian by myself, willingly this time. My paternal grandfather had passed away when I was in eleventh grade. I spent time with my father's brother Haywood and his wife, Betty, who radiates a calm that always balances my energy.

When I returned to Wesleyan, I sublet a room for a month while I worked for the University, painting dorm rooms. My African-American crush, Iju, was also on the painting crew. Still no interest.

On June 25, 1979, I created the following list:

My professional goal is to become a child psychologist.

Other major goals

- Understanding of God's teaching through Bible study
- Children's Theater Workshop—founding a black children's theater organization in Middletown, CT
- Semester in Paris (January to August 1980)
- Trip to Jamaica
- Top physical condition (weight around 135 lbs.)
- Becoming a true Christian
- Theater company at Wesleyan

At the time, everything on my list seemed reasonable. I had reached out to a children's theater professional in New York whom Esteban had referred me to for information on establishing a children's theater company. I would continue to work through my list.

In July, I worked as a Creative Theater Techniques teacher and counselor at the Center for Creative Youth. CCY was a residential arts program for students who had been identified as gifted and talented in music, dance, drama, vocal music, and visual arts— similar in focus to the Park Summer Arts program from my high school years, except these students were required to audition for slots in the various disciplines. I supervised a group of twelve girls, several of whom I grew close to, remaining in contact with them after the program ended.

I team-taught Creative Theater Techniques with two other counselors in the afternoons, leaving me time in the mornings to rest and think about the kind of person I wanted to be. I decided I wanted to exude compassion and to show forth love.

Each student was required to devise a project that they would implement in their high school during the upcoming school year. Inspired by that concept, I created a project combining theater techniques and literacy that I eventually executed at The Long Lane School in the spring semester of 1980.

In August, I participated in Wesleyan's residential Intensive Language Program (ILP), studying French. Planning to complete my application for Wesleyan's program in Paris in the fall, I needed additional language immersion. I had dreamed of studying in Paris since middle school. I completed the program successfully and was later selected for the study cohort that would convene in France from January to May 1980.

From summer 1978 to summer 1979, busier and more energetic than ever, I was calmer internally than I had ever been.

I believed those dreadful depressions were over forever.

CHAPTER FOURTEEN

"Obey them that have the rule over you, and submit yourselves; for they watch for your souls, as they that must give account, that they may do it with joy and not with grief: for that is unprofitable for you."
—BOOK OF HEBREWS 13–17

I FIRST VISITED New Born Church of God and True Holiness with Penny, on May 6, 1979, the first Sunday after her mother's homegoing. Ms. June passed away in April 1979. When she began attending this church in early spring, Penny had told me she thought I would really enjoy this loving congregation. That day, I came to support my grieving friend.

Truthfully, I had been looking for a church to attend on Sundays. The Catholic Church in Middletown was similar to the church of my early years—one step beyond the Latin mass. It was too dead for me. Though St. Ambrose celebrated a more traditional mass each week, I opted for the gospel mass at which I often sang on either the youth or adult choirs.

After being seated in the congregation of fifty or fewer saints, as the congregants called one another, I noticed a large sign on the rear wall of the pulpit at the front of the church. It read, simply, "God is Love." After the morning announcements, the pastor asked all visitors to stand, to be recognized by the congregation. I stood, along with four other people. When he asked if any visitor had anything to say, I responded, "I am delighted to be here. It seems like something exciting is going to happen here today." That was the improvisational theater performer in me speaking.

The preacher rendered a sermon entitled "A Common Temptation" about God's ability to help us overcome any obstacle. *Like depression*, I thought. His words reflected my concept of God: a loving father who provides a victorious life. After the sermon ended, as the choir sang something like, "Come unto Jesus, while you have time," the preacher invited people to come up to the altar for prayer. I lined up behind five or more people, sure that the preacher's prayer would be beneficial in some way.

While conferring with the minister, I decided to be baptized in Jesus' name. During the sermon, I learned purgatory wasn't biblical. The way I lived my life, replete with angry outbursts, which occasionally turned physical, I always figured I would need someone to pray me out of purgatory eventually. I didn't think I would commit any mortal sins for which the penalty would be hell. The Roman Catholic nuns from my elementary school made sure I absorbed the lessons regarding eternal life.

With purgatory off the table, I decided to take action. Knowing I had been merely sprinkled with water as a baby, I chose this baptism by complete immersion in water. When my friend Veda, who had met Mama, asked, "What are you going to tell your Catholic mother about being baptized?" I shrugged, then replied, "I'm not going to tell her."

That week, the Wesleyan spring semester ended. Although I had remained in Connecticut for the summer, my busy schedule only allowed me to attend two services at New Born: a Bible study in June and a Sunday morning worship service in July. When the pastor himself drove the half hour each way to make sure Penny and I could attend the service, I was impressed by his humility. This sacrificial attitude was what I had grown accustomed to in interactions with the clergy at St. Ambrose.

Wanting to know God more perfectly, I decided I really should attend church every week, as my mother had required of any child of hers who lived at her home in Baltimore. In September, I chose to settle in at this church along with my best friend, Penny. I could feel the genuine love the congregants shared with each other, and with me.

New Born Church of God exposed me to a new way of doing church. The church was patterned according to the Apostle's doctrine that included repentance, baptism, and receiving the Spirit of God as evidenced by speaking with supernatural tongues. The church embraced the basic tenets of early Pentecostalism in the

United States. In an effort to present ourselves in contrast to the world at large, we embraced standards of modesty with parameters that individual pastors determined.

In an effort to serve God perfectly, I followed instructions, initially those that pertained to how I dressed. As a college student, I wore sweatpants most days. After my baptism, I removed them and wore the same three skirts for a semester to conform to the requirement that sisters wear skirts and dresses. My lip gloss, eyeliner, and mascara became a thing of the past. When one of the mothers told me wearing nail polish was a sign of pride, I removed it, determined to line my life up with what I was told God required. Over the summer, I had decided I needed to add biblical salvation to my peaceful, happy life, making things better for me. If these new rules would help me become a more loving person, I would submit to them.

I decided my life shouldn't be about externals; I would concentrate on being a better person internally. If the Spirit of God would change me for the better, I needed to receive it. When I did, I was immediately faced with an important choice. I was accepted for the Wesleyan program in Paris for the spring semester. I had participated in the Wesleyan Intensive Language Program during the summer to prepare myself. Now I had to decide whether or not I possessed the spiritual strength necessary to make the trip while retaining my newfound fervor. When I talked to Penny about it, she suggested I ask God for a specific sign to signal his will, as Gideon had done when he was unsure about God's direction for his life. I didn't place a piece of sheepskin outdoors asking God to alternate wetting it one night and keeping it dry the other.

Knowing that money always fell in place for my scholastic endeavors, I decided I would leave the country if the finances for my trip were in place. I could not find funding to study in Paris.

After I decided to forego a major goal from my to-do and remain on campus, Penny shared, "Pastor Geddis told me not to tell you what to do about Paris. He said it needed to be your decision."

During winter break, I went to New Born Church of God in D.C. and stayed with Dee Dee, a sister from the church who was in her late twenties. She patiently shared her knowledge of God with me and radiated kindness. She invited me to ride to Tennessee for the revival her pastor Bishop Wilson was conducting. She served as his driver for that trip. As we rode through the West Virginia hills he pointed out the majesty of God. He also instructed me to memorize Galatians 2:20, which reads, "I am crucified with Christ: nevertheless I live; yet not I, but Christ liveth in me: and the life which I now live in the flesh I live by the faith of the Son of God, who loved me, and gave himself for me."

At home, my siblings commented on how plain looking I had become. I think this must have been a personal choice because one of the twenty-something sisters often reminded the sisterhood, "Holiness is not a synonym for homeliness." In my quest to be sober, I had lost effervescence as well as fashion sense without noticing.

Because I wanted to be a more loving person, I needed to work on my speech. Not how to speak, but rather what to say. I had always believed if I spoke the truth, people should accept whatever I said. I learned that wasn't so and that the childhood adage *sticks and stones may break my bone, but words can never hurt me* was untrue. I wanted to stop using hurtful speech. I decided if I was going to be a Christian ambassador, I needed to be genuine. I read books about getting better control of my tongue. To this day, I am really hurt when I unintentionally offend someone with words.

In February, our Church embarked on a month of Consecration, twenty-eight days to dedicate ourselves to God. I ate one meal a day as prescribed. Toward the middle of the month, one of the brothers invited Penny and me to his apartment for a home-cooked meal, which was delicious. A week later, out of nowhere, I called Dee Dee to let her know I would soon be engaged to that brother. She didn't challenge my assertion. However, she recognized a difference in my vocal tone that I didn't hear. She didn't believe what I was saying was true, nor did she think I was lying. She alerted my pastor.

Meanwhile, my thoughts began to race, and my speech and behavior began to speed up. My friend and fellow congregant, Bill, a doctoral candidate at Wesleyan, shared file cards with me on which he had written scriptures concerning Christian speech and behavior for me to meditate on. The uptick in my mood resulted in a loss of insight those cards could not restore.

That semester, I withdrew from three of my six classes. In my Psychology of Learning course, I gave a ten-minute extemporaneous discourse that no one understood, but the instructor allowed me to continue my nonsensical rant. Penny, a psychology major, found out about the strange discourse from another psychology major who had heard it. When she asked me about it, I had no explanation. What I said had made sense to me while I was speaking. Humiliated, I dropped the course.

I spent as much time as I could in my room reading my Bible and praying to try to slow down my racing thoughts.

I attended the church's all-night prayer service conducted from Friday night to Saturday morning in mid-February, thereby adding sleep deprivation to eating one meal a day and further interrupting the chemical functioning of my brain. On Saturday, I decided it was time to attend an on-campus party. I was extraordinarily cheerful, dancing to a few records before returning to my apartment.

Of course, being at a party was outside the parameters of my religious tenets. My pastor chided me for attending the party and for putting an earring in the piercing of my right ear. In response, I gathered all my jewelry, including an heirloom bracelet, and threw it into a garbage chute in my apartment building. It never occurred to me to hold onto it without wearing it until I could give it away. In my mood state, I thought throwing the jewelry away was my best shot at resisting the temptation to wear it.

In mid-March I plunged into a more ominous version of the depression of 1977. Throughout April, I was weepy and sad. I kept praying. Penny said, "It's a good thing you weren't at home with your family. They wouldn't have understood." How could they have understood something I didn't understand? At the time, I had no explanation for what was happening to me.

That semester, I designed two independent study courses at the Long Lane School, the juvenile detention facility for the state of Connecticut. I was teaching English and Creative Theater Techniques curriculums I designed to young men on the maximum-security unit. When hypomania kicked in, I manifested a new seductiveness that became counterproductive. One of the counselors warned me that my behavior was too provocative for this population. I mustered enough clarity to know I needed to leave that ward.

With heightened persuasive abilities, I was able to rescue my project by appealing to the head of the girls' division who allowed me to switch my attention to a group of girls in the minimum-detention section of the facility. I tutored English and taught them how to turn their dreams into stories they acted out. I recorded my experiences in one journal for the English professor who was overseeing my work and another journal for the theater professor who monitored the theater component.

Penny and Bill graduated from Wesleyan in May. To celebrate her accomplishment, Penny and I decided to travel from New York to California where we would stay with one of her friends. We traveled to parts of the country I had never visited, passing through Arizona's fresh air, seeing the Saint Louis arch at dusk—every new state provided its own beauty. But after two days, it seemed the bus trip would never end and our feet were swollen. After arriving in California, we decided to fly back home. Penny had enough money to buy a ticket, but my refunded bus ticket money was not enough for a plane ticket. I borrowed the remainder of the money I needed from Karen, promising to pay it back later that summer.

When we returned to Connecticut, Penny suffered whiplash in a van accident and wasn't able to work. Covering the rent, I couldn't afford to pay Karen back in the timeframe we had established. It took much longer to pay her back than I expected. She promised she would never loan me money again.

In July, I went home to have my bridesmaid gown fitted for Valerie's upcoming wedding and bridal shower. I returned in August for the wedding. Penny and one of the other sisters from church attended the wedding with me. My pastor suggested I skip my sister's wedding reception to attend a church service my congregation attended in D.C. that day. I let him know I planned to celebrate with my sister and our family on her special day. Though, I wanted to create a new life for myself in the Pentecostal faith, I would always participate in major family events. There was no way I would be off somewhere at a church service when my sister was beginning a new chapter in her life.

CHAPTER FIFTEEN

"Do you know what happens when dreams cannot get out?"
—MERRICK, THE ELEPHANT MAN
(BERNARD POMERANCE'S
THE ELEPHANT MAN)

By the fall of 1980, I no longer felt the internal freedom theater had given me, nor was I walking in the joy I derived from my initial salvation experience of November 1979. As I think back, I had become enslaved to rules, judgments, and traditions no one explained to me. I just accepted them—even those that seemed arbitrary—because at the time, I thought they were essential to salvation.

Penny moved in with one of the sisters and her children in New Britain. For the first few weeks of the semester, I would spend Sunday night there, returning to Middletown in time for my class on Monday evening. Not wanting to inconvenience the woman Penny roomed with any longer, Penny started bringing me home on Sunday nights. My old roommate Michelle and I were roommates again at the William Street high-rise. On the weekends she went out of town, I would sleep in her room, allowing Penny to stay in mine.

This semester, I took two English courses, a religion course, and two theatre courses. I studied standard stage diction and began writing a play to be performed at the student-run '92 Theater during the spring semester. I loved studying voice and learning how to care for my vocal instrument more effectively. I felt a little uncomfortable lying on the floor wearing skirts and wondered if my sweats-clad classmates found my attire strange, but I made it work. With my play unfinished by the end of the semester, I deferred my grade.

I spent part of the semester pursuing a young man from church who described me as, "a rushing mighty wind." *I was drawn to him because he loved the Lord*, I reasoned. I was more attracted to his need for nurturance. His lack of interest answered the question from *for colored girls* regarding whether or not "I could stand not being wanted when I wanted to be wanted." Like the lady in red, I decided I could not. However, I felt punted in no predetermined direction, as a football kicked by a young child.

In early December, a friend from a church we fellowshipped with just outside Boston invited me to spend a couple of days with her. Bishop Wilson was preaching there for a few nights, and the saints from my church would be coming to Saturday's service. I arranged a ride back to Connecticut in the church's van. One of the brothers from my church, a Harvard law student, offered to give me a campus tour. While there, I visited the English department to get information about the graduate program. I didn't plan to apply, but the visit gave me assurance I could succeed in the Harvard intellectual community had I chosen that path.

My friend's roommate had been a professional modern dancer before joining their Apostolic Church. In conformance with the no worldly pursuits tenet of Pentecostalism, she had abandoned dance. I think she found a job in an office instead. Something clicked, or rather, erupted in my head. Her happiness with her decision gave me pause as I questioned whether or not theatrical studies were in sync with my new lifestyle. *Should I be a theater major?* was my internal question. My mind fought the possibility of God requiring me to give up drama to serve Him more perfectly. Then again, I was determined to walk according to the Master's plan, whatever that might be.

The night my congregation was expected for service, my friend's pastor announced that an emergency had forced the saints from Connecticut to forego the service, leaving me without transportation back to school. I had five dollars. When it was time to collect the church offering, I put all of my money in seed money, in Apostolic parlance. It was not enough to get home. I said a prayer in my head, asking for the situation to work favorably for me.

At the end of the service, after greeting Bishop Wilson, I

explained my quandary. "I'll take you back to Connecticut, daughter," he assured me. I knew him fairly well, having ridden in Dee Dee's car with him on our road trip to Tennessee during my Christmas break in 1979.

It was the end of the semester. When I came home from Massachusetts, I had a few days to write a paper for each of the two English classes I was taking. My mind whirled with thoughts of whether or not studying theater lined up with salvation, I got no schoolwork accomplished. The instructors granted me incompletes for each of those classes.

I planned to go home briefly for the Christmas holiday before returning to spend the second half of my vacation with the saints. I would stay with my pastor and his family. On the Friday before Christmas, one of the brothers came to drive me from Middletown to New Britain. I only needed to pack my clothes. Instead, an unknown inner force compelled me to pack up my apartment, including the pots, pans and dishes. Because it took extra time to load everything in the car, we were late for church.

As often happened, in deference to my dramatic flair, I was called forward to do a reading. Rather than read a religious poem, as usual, I chose the 'measure him right' speech from *A Raisin in the Sun*, reading with an accusatory tone.

At Sunday morning service, I grabbed one of the tambourines from a pew and played it during testimony service. Never competent with a tambourine before, it seemed I had suddenly become a skilled percussionist. And when the preacher delivered the morning message, I recorded as much of it as I could in long hand, like a stenographer would, not wanting to miss the extraordinary message I believed the Lord was communicating directly to me.

CHAPTER SIXTEEN

"To the person in the bell jar, blank and stopped as a dead baby, the world itself is the bad dream."

—SYLVIA PLATH (*THE BELL JAR*)

THE NEXT DAY, Monday, December 22, 1980, I had a train to catch. It was exactly one week after my twenty-first birthday. That day, I had called Mama to thank her for being a terrifically supportive mother. Since returning from my trip to Massachusetts, my speech had become schmaltzy and even slightly maudlin. I outdid myself as I praised her.

When one of the brothers arrived to drive me to the train, I was not ready, having unnecessarily pulled things from my suitcase. I grabbed the sack of presents I bought for my siblings—new bibles—along with the suitcase I hurriedly repacked. By the time we arrived at the Berlin station, the train was pulling away. My driver told me not to worry, he was going to drive to the next station. I would catch that train home. Grabbing the steering wheel, he sped away from the station with the determination of a NASCAR driver. We arrived in Meriden just before the train pulled up and I was able to board safely. My escort was visibly relieved.

Having missed breakfast, I went to the café car to purchase a hot ham and cheese sandwich. For the holidays, I supposed, there were cute little baskets filled with meats, cheeses and crackers available. I bought one along with my sandwich, chips, and Sprite. I returned to my seat to eat my meal. *What will I do with the snacks in this basket?* I wondered. I decided to pass them out to strangers seated in my railcar. I had to say something as I proffered each treat. In the holiday spirit, I settled on, "If you meet me and forget me you have lost nothing. If you meet Jesus and forget him, you have lost everything." I had seen it written on a card. People looked at me quizzically, but smiled and accepted the snacks, anyway. As I made my way through the car, I was assisted by a six-year-old girl who asked permission from her mother. She held the basket from which I pulled the gifts.

Proud of my ability to spread cheer, I returned to the café car for another basket of snacks. The little girl wanted to help me again. This time, her mother refused her request, having processed the erratic quality of my behavior. They got off the train in New York. For the rest of the trip home, I chatted with an older African-American gentleman who was traveling to Washington, D.C. for the holiday. I changed seats to sit next to him after spying him in the car. Noticing the point on my pencil was broken, I challenged him to sharpen it without a pencil sharpener. He did it using a pen knife.

I took a cab home from the train station and spent several days with my family before returning to New Britain. Although my brain has blocked my memory of that visit, I remember my behavior being erratic. Many years later, I asked Mama how she had allowed me to return to Connecticut in such an exaggerated mood. She remembered asking me to remain in Baltimore, but she believed, as an adult, I was free to make my own decisions.

I returned to New Britain in a clearly hypomanic state. At the time, the people I was around had no understanding of my behavior. They were surprised my family allowed me to return. I arrived in the evening. After twenty-four hours at her house, my pastor's wife confronted me. My behavior was scaring her. She told me, "I am not going to allow you to disrupt my household." I told her I would leave.

My pastor, who I had never seen come upstairs in my many overnight stays at their home, came upstairs to calm me. All I retained from his admonition was the scripture, "A man's gift will make room for him and bring him before great men."

Adamant about leaving, I convinced one of the brothers from church to drive me to Leslie's house in Middletown. She was surprised to see me. Good friends in our early Wesleyan years, we had very little contact since my New Born transition. This was my first visit to this residence. I am not sure how I knew where she lived. When I arrived, she had me sit down at her kitchen table and made me a cup of hot tea. Calm, balanced Leslie appeared troubled by my exaggerated, irritable mood. Her mother, Mrs. Jones, a psychologist, sat with us in the kitchen. She was visiting her daughter for the holidays.

The next thing I remember is being in the emergency room at Middlesex Memorial Hospital in Middletown. Then my father arrived. He later told me he believed someone from the University called with details of my location. He arrived by train, planning to take me home. When he came into the room, I was telling him how I had found Hemingway's clean, well-lighted place, insisting he concur. I also shared I was engaged to one of Penny's brothers. Not so. He and I had a discussion about the Quran just before Christmas, making him as good a candidate as any for the boyfriend/husband role, a staple in my manic improvisations. A doctor talked to me and tested my reflexes in my father's presence. I had become physically stronger than usual and was very energetic, nearly bouncing around the examining room where I had been corralled.

My father petitioned the doctor to sedate me enough for him to get me home. The psychiatrist informed my dad I was suffering with manic-depression, now termed bipolar disorder. I was too sick to travel. In my mental state, I posed a threat to myself and others. Two doctors would be signing me into the state psychiatric facility for observation and treatment. My father was powerless; there was nothing he could do.

Meanwhile, back in New Britain, Pastor Geddis, chaplain at New Britain General Hospital, secured a bed for me at that facility. Penny remained in New Britain, awaiting my arrival. She called Leslie and relayed this information so she could pass it along to my father. I pieced the commitment debacle together over the years based on Penny's and Daddy's recollections. My dad, who later expressed being disappointed by Penny's absence in Middletown, never saw Leslie, only her mother. I doubt Mrs. Jones knew anything about the New Britain hospital arrangement.

My dad remembers a Mrs. Olson, who talked soothingly to him and got him some milk to drink as he waited for his baby to be transported to the psychiatric institution. He was unable to summon the calm he had exhibited when my grandmother was ill. He returned to Baltimore the following day. Alone. Maybe things would have been different had I gone to New Britain General Hospital.

I was given an injection of Haldol to sedate me for my trip to Connecticut Valley Hospital, formerly Connecticut General Hospital for the Insane. Wesleyan students knew it as CVH. Though it was the other beautiful campus in Middletown, nobody wished to end up there. When I awakened at CVH, I was lying straitjacketed on a table in a pool of my own urine. When I gained consciousness earlier, I had fought the techs and needed to be restrained. I was restrained again the following day when my fight reflex kicked in again as a nurse tried to administer a Haldol injection by needle. This second time, I retained control of my bladder. For the next several days, refusing to take medicine by mouth, I was held down and given injections in my buttocks. I finally relented and received medication orally.

Hearing of my whereabouts, my former roommate Michelle traveled to the hospital from New York. Her mother was a nurse, but I do not know how she recognized I was experiencing a negative reaction to Navane, the psychotropic medicine being administered to me. I was having difficulty speaking and I was drooling. In her characteristically authoritative manner, she told the nurse that administration of the drug Navane would need to be discontinued. The doctor stopped the medicine at her insistence. The hospital staff had seemed oblivious to the side effects the drug caused.

One of the social workers at CVH identified herself as an Apostolic minister. When I had become calmer, she would sometimes take me to wards where she was assigned. I'm certain she was praying for me.

Penny visited every day but one, when it was bitterly cold. My pastor and several of the saints visited as well. Unlike many other fundamentalists living in the United States in the early 1980s, Bishop Geddis saw bipolar disorder as an illness, not a demon that needed to be cast out. Before I went back to Baltimore after the CVH commitment, Bishop Geddis had reasoned, "This is an illness that needs to be treated. If you had a toothache, you would go to a dentist, wouldn't you?" His encouragement did not erase my personal shame. I secretly categorized myself as crazy, but it was mildly comforting to know someone I respected did not.

THE SECOND WEEK of my commitment, when I was coming down from my unwelcomed high, I remember being allowed to walk alone outside in the afternoons. I would repeat Isaiah 40:31 to myself: "But they that wait upon the Lord shall renew their strength; they shall mount up with wings as eagles; they shall run, and not be weary, and they shall walk, and not faint." I had to believe God was going to release me from this waking nightmare.

Penny wrote me a letter during my confinement that included the line, "Come on back to reality, Ri." Eventually, with divine assistance, I did.

CHAPTER SEVENTEEN

"If you're going through hell, keep going."
—WINSTON CHURCHILL

UNLIKE DEPRESSIONS I had suffered, mania terrified me. The improvisational behavior I had recently exhibited lacked the control of classic theatrical improvisation. I was used to being directed by a brain that processed my actions before I performed them. While manic, I did whatever came next without making certain it was grounded in reality, and that was *crazy*. This was especially frightening for me because my self image was largely based on intellectual achievement and self-control. Other than Bishop Geddis, no one around me seemed to understand my symptoms as manifestations of an illness.

After I was forcibly medicated out of the unwelcome high, a doctor at CVH recommended I take lithium, a naturally occurring salt on the periodic table, in a concentrated dose to quell the mania. While considering his advice, I met a young woman at the hospital whose behavior seemed extremely erratic, even while taking lithium. Not knowing it takes time for the medication to work effectively, I decided lithium was not for me and refused the drug. Unfortunately, as a twenty-two-year-old adult in charge of my own medical decisions, I didn't seek outside counsel. After fifteen days, when my mood stabilized, I was discharged with instructions to take a multi-vitamin. Two female workers at the facility admonished me, separately, not to come back to the facility, as if being at a *looney farm* was my choice.

After my refusal to be medicated, I left Connecticut Valley Hospital thinking I was probably insane but hoping the episodic mania had been an anomaly.

Penny picked me up from the institution and drove me to my apartment. When I met with Dr. Coughlin, who I hadn't conferred with in person since my return to Wesleyan in 1978, she told me I needed another semester off to allow my mind to rest. That would put me a full year behind my entering class at Wesleyan. Not happy about being a slow finisher, I appeased myself with the assurance of returning to graduate with the class of 1982. Because I had packed up most of my things and stored them at my pastor's house in December, I only had to take my clothing home. I left my books in storage, but never retrieved them, not remembering where they were. Through the years I've lost a variety of possessions during manias.

Penny drove me to the train station. As we said goodbye, she looked apprehensive. I was definitely not the bubbly woman she traveled cross-country with on the bus trip on which I read my Random House pocket dictionary recreationally. I assured her I would be back. At least, that was my hope.

Before going home, I called my pastor's wife to apologize for the ways my manic behavior had disrupted the peace in her home. A couple of years later, she wrote me a note asking me to forgive her if any of her actions had caused my condition to worsen. She assured me that was never her intent.

When I arrived back home, I wrote in my journal, *I am feeling so paralyzed that I have to force myself to do the simplest things, like getting up and getting dressed.* My sister Valerie, who talks far less than I, called me everyday to make sure I had a conversation with somebody. Thanks to my six years of indoctrination by the School Sisters of Notre Dame, suicide was still off the table.

When I felt well enough to speak to someone outside my family, I called Dee Dee to relate what happened. Rather than speak by phone, she invited me to visit at her home in D.C. While there, I had a conference with Bishop Wilson, our organization's overseer, at their church. I imagined Bishop Geddis had already recounted my story. Bishop Wilson sat at his desk, with me seated in a chair opposite him. Establishing eye contact with me, he questioned, "What happened, Daughter?" Emotionally exhausted, I related how thoughts sped up in my head after he dropped me off at school, and I eventually ended up committed to a psychiatric facility for fifteen days.

"I'm better now, not taking any medication," I declared. After he listened to my tale of psychiatric imprisonment. I shared the conclusion I had reached for my future.

Feeling no Spirit-filled saint should go through what I just had, I decided studying theater was destroying me; it was my mammon. I reasoned that abandoning theater was my solution. Knowing Jesus said no one could serve God and mammon, I refused to be an idolater. Back then, unaware of my confusion, no one explained mammon was the Greek word for money.

Bishop Geddis discouraged worldly entertainment. He encouraged his flock to carefully monitor television viewing, referring to TV as "the one-eyed demon."

Having thought this new teaching through, I concluded, "If you can't go to movies and plays, and your TV viewing is limited, you certainly can't pursue acting or directing, as you had planned." So, wanting to be the best Christian possible, circa 1906, the spread of early Pentecostalism in the United States, I erroneously concluded God wanted me to forsake theater, the pursuit that had nourished my spirit.

Bishop Wilson listened, respecting my right to make my own life choice. I do not remember him saying yea or nay to my decision. At this time no one, including me, understood theater was the thing God sent into my life to nourish my soul. I decided that although it was a fine pursuit for a Catholic, I needed to embrace the sober mindedness befitting my Apostolic lifestyle. This was an erroneous and harmful conclusion. However, no one in my Pentecostal world possessed the wisdom and understanding necessary to assure me that theatrical pursuits nurtured me. I replaced theatrical nurturance with spiritual anesthesia.

CHAPTER EIGHTEEN

*"Nay, let them only see us while
We wear the mask."*
—PAUL LAURENCE DUNBAR

To ease my feelings of humiliation, I chose to treat this semester off as a sabbatical. If I was going to be the best Christian me, I needed to belong to a church congregation where I would have a temporary pastor. I became an adjunct member of Calvary Church of Jesus Christ in Baltimore, the church I first visited with Dee Dee in December 1979 at Bishop Wilson's recommendation. Having no transportation to D.C., he believed Bishop Byron's church, which was not a member of the New Born Church Organization, would be suitable for Christian fellowship whenever I visited Baltimore.

Our neighbor Mrs. Dixon drove me to Tuesday night prayer service in late January. I was glad to be in a church that had corporate prayer, a service where everyone in the congregation spends an hour kneeling in prayer.

I met with Bishop Byron and talked to him about my recent psychiatric commitment. He connected me to a sister in the assembly who worked in a psychiatric institution. She encouraged me to call her as needed. I was thankful for her insightful listening. During this sabbatical, these were the only people at United to whom I revealed my commitment at Connecticut Valley Hospital.

This congregation was an outgrowth of Church of the Lord Jesus Christ. I noted the doctrinal teachings of this congregation, comparing them to New Born in Connecticut. Saints were encouraged to develop faith in God, to pray and to fast at both congregations. In Baltimore, the sisters were prohibited from chemically straightening their hair, as mine was; their skirts were required to fall below the calf, while mine were over the knee. The colors orange and red were considered too loud for the saints, and red was my favorite color. Sisters wore no jewelry, not even wedding rings. In Connecticut, the sisters wore brooches and class rings. Wedding rings were definitely worn.

Combining Paul's admonishment that women cover their heads while praying with the scriptures that encourage saints to pray continually, sisters were instructed to wear head coverings constantly. Some of the older women wore turbans or scarves at all times, only removing them to wash their hair. This struck me as extreme and unnecessary.

I asked Bishop Byron about movie and theater attendance; they were taboo here also. These saints were allowed to bowl and roller skate, which were New Born taboos. I remembered what Penny told me about each pastor setting parameters for his congregation. *Should I try to comply?*

My friend Bill had moved from Connecticut to D.C. after earning his doctorate from Wesleyan in 1979. Having suffered a nervous breakdown pre-salvation, he empathized with me. We spoke by phone several times, and then he visited me at home. As we sat in the park behind my house, with my head covered, I told him about United. The preaching was fine and I loved the hymns we sang, but I could not understand the rationale behind the dress code for sisters.

I asked him, "Bill, the Bible says if the Son makes you free, you'll be free indeed. Why do I feel so bound?"

We discussed my question, then he suggested, "Maybe this isn't the right church for you." Maybe it wasn't, but I'd be leaving in August. At that point in early spring, I lacked the energy it would take to find a church.

I went to the outpatient psychiatry department at Sinai where I met with a therapist for a couple of months. We discussed how I felt about my confinement at Connecticut Valley Hospital and whether or not I felt the mania would recur. I did not.

I got a temp job at Johns Hopkins University. I started as a file clerk in the payroll department, then transferred to the accounts payable department to microfilm the university's paid bills and research bill payment histories saved to microfilm and microfiche. It was as exciting as it sounds. I welcomed the monotony.

On Sundays, I went to morning service, came home for dinner, and returned for evening service by bus. My sister Ernestine often accompanied me, like a family bodyguard. One Sunday in early March, I suggested we turn around and go back home rather than walk to the bus. Feeling overwhelmed, I thought, *This isn't working. It might be time for me to give up on salvation.* If I went home at that moment, I would have abandoned the Apostolic faith. As if she could read my thoughts, my sister declared, "You'll feel better if you go to the service." Knowing she was right, we continued on to the bus stop.

I enjoyed fellowship with the saints at Calvary for the next several months, without anyone uncovering my hidden mental instability. I made a couple of friends who provided the human connection I needed within the congregation. I was unwilling to face the undeniable stigma associated with my illness. During my Baltimore tenure, I endured preachers insisting that born-again believers did not suffer mental illness. They reasoned that mental illness was a sign of demonic possession, sighting the demoniac of Gadara who dwelled naked in the tombs cutting himself, possessed by devils before Jesus healed him. In their vernacular, "the demon of mental illness could never affect a blood-washed saint. Fasting and prayer would drive any demon far from you." Fortunately, I had learned at New Born that a demonic spirit trying to repress me could never possess me as a possessor of God's spirit.

Was this the atmosphere in which I could discuss having a chemically imbalanced brain?

One Tuesday night at prayer service, I knelt for a conversation with God. In my head, I prayed: *Lord, if what happened to me in December is ever going to happen to me again, please kill me before it does.* This was the closest I came to suicidal ideation.

Thank you, School Sisters of Notre Dame.

CHAPTER NINETEEN

"Life itself is a drama in various acts"

—ANONYMOUS, AS SHARED BY CHERYL STEVENS

In late August 1981, still alive, I returned to Wesleyan and my New Born church family, where I would not have to expend psychic energy guarding my secret. Dr. Coughlin readmitted me from my involuntary leave of medical absence to begin my senior year in Middletown.

My new roommate, Jackie, and I shared a university owned apartment—a third floor walk-up—in a house on High Street. Both of us were members of New Born Church of God and True Holiness.

Because I had taken two separate semesters of medical leave since entering Wes U in 1977, most students I knew well had graduated in May of 1981 or earlier. At this point, it didn't matter. Since getting saved at New Born in November 1979, my interests had shifted away from on-campus life. My life was much different than it had been in the summer of 1979—unbalanced rather than peaceful.

I knew people who went to college and morphed from straight-laced geeks without any social life to all-the-way live partiers. My transition was pretty much the opposite. I arrived at Wesleyan as the gregarious, improvisational theater performer who spiked the punch with grain alcohol for the freshman party I organized at the Malcolm X house.

In the absence of campus sororities, a group of girlfriends and I launched a sisterhood we called I Phelta Thi. We created an anthem based on the refrain of the song, "Bustin' Loose." It went, "I feel like feeling a thigh / I felt a thigh." As we chanted, we'd touch some random male student's leg. All in good fun. As I sought more spiritual depth, I abandoned my free-spirited partying lifestyle. It wasn't in sync with my newly learned concept of sober-mindedness.

While living on High Street, I attended classes on campus

during the week. I spent the greater part of my weekends at church, attending services on Friday nights, Sunday mornings, and Sunday evenings. I occasionally attended prayer on Saturday afternoon, as well. Our assistant pastor drove to the Wesleyan campus on Wednesday evenings to lead the in-depth Bible study I loved.

As a result of those teachings, I learned the importance of studying and internalizing scripture in order to lead a fulfilled life. I also reabsorbed the necessity of looking for the good in others. After all, I was the young woman whose senior yearbook page included a Confucius quote, "Everything has its beauty, but not everyone sees it."

When I first began attending New Born regularly in September 1979, I learned the scriptural admonition, "Not forsaking the assembling of yourselves together, as the manner of some is." The thought, *this church schedule is a bit excessive*, lingered in my mind, but I eventually accepted this regimentation as a necessary part of our congregational culture. Knowing a little more about holiness than I, Penny shared that each pastor set up rules to best serve the entire membership. I trusted my pastor's judgment. I wouldn't learn until many years later that some of our dogma was simply rooted in Pentecostal traditionalism.

My family knew I had changed religious affiliation, but they had no idea how often I went to church. I didn't tell them. My conversion was too soon after the Jim Jones debacle in which the cult's leader convinced his membership to commit suicide en masse by drinking poisoned Kool-Aid. I didn't want them to think I had joined a cult. Karen often encouraged me to "return to the faith of our fathers." Knowing I often pursued new endeavors in two-year blocks, she figured I'd abandon this new religion soon.

Academically, I majored in English. My original double major was Psychology and Theater. Psychology was not a fit for me. I was a little disappointed when it didn't work out. My mom had intimated she wanted to study child psychology in college. It would have been gratifying to achieve her goal. In the 1940s, a college instructor suggested she become a teacher or a nurse, appropriate jobs for professional colored women of that day. Dutifully, she became an elementary school teacher.

I had excelled in one psychology course, Dramaturgical Approaches to the Study of Psychology, because it was a theater class—a natural fit for me. Of course, I dropped my theater major after becoming a fundamentalist Christian.

In February 1982, before I understood the necessity of eating regularly, sleeping restfully, and remaining stress free for stable mental health, I embarked on a month of consecration with my church congregation. I ate and drank once a day at dinnertime. During that time, a religious station in Hartford, CT requested an interview at the station to talk about our local congregation. My pastor chose me to discuss our church's teachings on the air. Because I was a well-balanced, articulate college student, he trusted me to give a well-rounded description of our congregational beliefs and practices. With my mood escalating, my interview responses were pretty much in your face.

Meanwhile, I continued my class regimen, determined to earn a degree in English in May 1982. Hopefully, by that time, I would be offered a job in close proximity to my new church family.

CHAPTER TWENTY

"Make peace with your past."

—MIRIAM STOFFELS

FOR ME, MARCH 1982 will always mark the point when the royal hues of my life's tapestry faded to grays. Perhaps that is why I remember these events vividly.

By the first Wednesday in March, I lurched into a familiar exhaustion. That evening, I lacked the energy to walk the four blocks to the William Street high rise where we held our Bible studies. Wanting to familiarize myself with God's Word, I never missed Bible study. Although Jackie—I called her "Boo"—wasn't exactly sure what was wrong, she sensed something was off with me. She asked if I was all right, then attended Bible study without me.

A couple of hours later, she returned to our apartment with our Bible study leader, his wife, and our friends Penny and Ron in tow. She had asked them to come and pray with me. After prayer, she and Penny suggested I drink hot chamomile tea, which always soothed me, before bedtime. I did as they suggested, and then drank some ginger ale to soothe the odd feeling in the pit of my stomach. Having changed into my nightgown, I lay down, but didn't fall asleep. I got back up and returned to the kitchen for some Skippy peanut butter. Eating a single spoon of smooth peanut butter directly out of the jar had soothed me since childhood. As a child, I regularly snuck spoonsfuls from the jar in the kitchen cabinet.

Returning to bed, I burrowed under my covers and fell into a deep sleep. I was wide-awake at six in the morning, earlier than usual. I placed the pillow over my face and tried to go back to sleep. After an hour of hyper-wakefulness, I decided to soak in the tub, to quiet my restlessness. That usually helped when I felt wired, as I did this particular morning. Out of the tub I got dressed and made myself some scrambled eggs and buttered toast. After eating, I noted yesterday's wave of enervation had passed. I now felt extraordinarily energized. I decided to bake brownies. *I'll need to go to the store. I can just skip class this morning,* I told myself. Ordinarily, I was not one to skip classes.

I waited for the store to open and walked, almost skipping, to the market six blocks away. I brought brownie mix, eggs, and apples up to the register, where I grabbed a glasses repair kit. *Can you have too many eyeglass repair kits?* I asked myself as I handed it to the cashier. My thoughts continued, *Would it have been on display at this particular register if I didn't need it?*

When I got back to the apartment, before putting the groceries away, I saw a small spill on a refrigerator shelf. I decided to completely clean out the refrigerator. This was usually Jackie's job, but when I feel stressed, I clean—a habit I developed as a child. I removed every container stored inside, then wiped out the inside of the refrigerator with warm, soapy water before replacing the contents, neatly.

When I finished, it was twelve noon. At that time, every weekday, Jackie and I prayed together for about a half hour. Some of our fellow campus Christians routinely joined us as we prayed in our cozy living room. This Thursday, Ron joined us for a prayer, and I prayed in an unusually loud voice. When prayer was over, Jackie turned to me and asked, with what seemed to me to be unwarranted concern, "How are you feeling, RiRi?"

I guessed she had noticed the fridge. "Great. Never better," I exclaimed.

Ron questioned, "Are you sure?"

"Of course, why wouldn't I be?" I asked. Jackie left to go to work at the library.

Like most days, Ron stayed for lunch with me after prayer ended. This day, he made himself a ham and provolone sandwich on a Kaiser roll and drank some juice. As we both ate lunch, I noticed him looking at me with concern, like Jackie had looked at me after prayer. Before leaving, he grabbed an apple, then gazed at me intently, instructing, "If you need me, call the house. Leave a message if I'm not there."

"Okay," I responded, wondering why he was saying this to me instead of his usual, "See you later," or "Praise Him."

When Ron left, I washed our dishes, then went in the living room to read a book. For my senior English tutorial, I was writing a short story collection. As I wrote, I read books by published authors, studying their craft. That day, I was reading Zora Neale Hurston's *Moses, Man of the Mountain*, absorbing her exquisite use of dialect. Jackie got home in time to make dinner, her delectable liver and onions. While she made dinner in our eat-in kitchen, I finally made the brownies.

Ron showed up for dinner. He had run into Jackie at the library while she was working. She told him to come over for his favorite meal. He always said he never liked liver before sampling Jackie's. His visit served two purposes. I knew he was also checking on me. All through the meal, I'd catch him scrutinizing me. *Why?* I wondered. After dinner, he asked if I was feeling better. "I feel terrific," I answered, with gusto. He gave me what I would call a concerned hug before leaving. A pre-med student, he had to go read reserve articles in the science library. Jackie went to her room. It was my turn to wash and put away the dishes.

We had leftover brownies. An idea struck me, *why not give them to the guys who lived on the second floor?* I decided that they would probably *love* to have those delicious brownies. Did it matter I had only spoken to them in passing since moving to High Street? But, of the four, I did know one of their names. After a few moments, I marched down the outdoor back steps with the brownies on a paper plate I had neatly covered in plastic wrap in my right hand. In my left hand, I carried a smallish, portable cassette player. They were glad to accept the treats, but unprepared when I decided to play the game "Who sang it best?" with them, a game I had just made up before leaving the kitchen. The two young men who were home ate brownies and listened while I played two renditions of the same gospel song for them.

"After hearing both versions," I challenged, "you will decide which you liked better." Before playing anything, I shared my opinion. "I like the version from my church choir better than the professional choir. It sounds more anointed." Mind you, I'm speaking to young, upper middle-class frat boys from Massachusetts. They definitely seemed bemused.

When Jackie came into the kitchen to get a drink from the fridge, she noticed the open back door. Looking down the stairs and taken aback by my unusual behavior, she rescued our neighbors from me. "Ri, I need you in the house." Bidding my friends adieu, I skipped up the steep steps like a gazelle and returned to the kitchen. After locking the door behind us, Jackie, who had a proverbial steel-trap memory, claimed she no longer remembered what she wanted. *Why is Boo acting so strangely?* I wondered. I read more of my book, aloud, in a stage whisper. After another shower, I decided to work on a short story before bed. Most nights, my mind shut down at eleven. That night, I wrote and read without sleeping.

Early Friday morning, I took a shower to energize myself. I ate oatmeal and a banana. I drank some juice. I felt like visiting. Upon leaving my apartment, I walked up High Street and turned down William Street. While approaching the high rise, I saw Terry, an African-American woman I knew slightly, as she entered the building. I called out for her to hold the door and engaged her in what I considered scintillating conversation while she waited for the elevator. As co-chair of the Fellows Dining Program, a weekly dining experience for faculty and African-American students, I was familiar with most of the black students on campus. I sometimes popped in for visits with African-American students when I passed their rooms.

This day, my energy was different, more ebullient. "Terry," I bubbled, while she waited for the elevator, "You're just the person I was hoping to see today." Actually, I would have expressed this sentiment to anyone I had seen standing at that door.

She invited me up to her apartment. We sat at her kitchen table, discussing the upcoming spring break. I told her about the fictional trip I was planning for break. I thought the trip was real. Before I left, I borrowed her garment bag, promising to return it after I returned to campus. As I carried the bag up the hill, in my mind, it transformed from an ordinary suitcase to a special prize. As in any great improvisation, I was incorporating ideas quickly.

After placing the bag in my room, I felt driven to check my P.O box at the university post office even though my mail now came directly to my High Street address. By this time, I had missed prayer. Furthermore, I hadn't let Jackie know where I was going when I left that morning. We usually informed one another of our whereabouts as a safety precaution. When I got back, Jackie's concern seemed to become more solicitous. When she asked if I was okay, I assured her I was fine. I decided to stay home from church that night, citing the fact I hadn't slept well the night before. I took a shower and deep cleaned the bathroom while Jackie was gone. I drank chamomile tea. When I heard Jackie on the stairs around eleven, I went in my room and closed the door.

I said goodnight to her through my bedroom door. I'm sure I sounded as wide awake as I was. She said she was tired and going to bed. She didn't knock lightly on my door as she normally would, so I could invite her to open the door to speak face to face. That was strange to me. When I heard her close her door for the night,

I came back into the living room to make calls from our phone that sat atop the living room bookcase, just outside her bedroom door. I stayed up making random phone call after phone call. And, as Mama always said, my voice carries. That was her nice way of saying I cannot whisper.

After a couple of hours, Jackie opened her door and said, "Ri, I need you to stop talking. I can't sleep." I apologized. She went back to bed. I made another call. After about a half hour or so, a very tired Jackie returned to the living room and asked to use the phone. I gave it to her. It was now around two in the morning. I heard her explaining my excessive phone use to our Bible study leader. She asked him, "What should I do?" She listened to his response, said goodbye, placed the phone on the hook, unplugged it, and wrapped the cord around it. She instructed me to stay in the apartment, something she had never said to me before. Then she took the phone into her bedroom and closed her door. For me, it was as if she had slammed the door in my face.

I went into the bathroom and took a bath, hoping the warm water would induce sleep. Without the phone, I took *Mules and Men* into the kitchen, flipping through the pages. Although it was becoming harder to understand what I was reading, I read and ate granola. Of course, then I had to I brush my teeth. I lay on my bed, listening to instrumental music in an unsuccessful attempt to still the rapid-fire, flight-of-ideas thought process that had begun, preventing sleep.

Around nine that morning, when Jackie came out of her bedroom, she asked if I had slept. "No. I can't." I moaned. Jackie retrieved the phone from her bedroom, plugged it back into the wall, and called Penny. My best friend, Penny was the right person to call. And she had lived through this behavior with me before.

Jackie detailed my activity, "Pen, Ri didn't sleep again last night.

Like I told you yesterday. I don't think she's had any sleep since Wednesday night. I don't know what to do. She was up, talking on the phone at two o'clock this morning. You know she's barely functional past midnight. When I couldn't sleep, I actually prayed she would stop, but she kept talking. Even after I told her she was keeping me up. I called Elder and asked him what I should do. He suggested I unplug the phone. So I did and placed it in a drawer in my room, where she couldn't get it. When I woke up this morning, she was still awake. Penny, I need you to come to Middletown," she pleaded, "I don't know what to do." She then added, "I can't leave Ri here by herself."

She sent one of her friends to find Cheryl, my closest friend on campus.

Once Cheryl and Penny arrived that Saturday, they stayed with me all day while I yammered away, jumping from one topic to another. Any thought that came to mind spilled from my mouth. Of course, I talked to them about my writing and about Zora Neale Hurston and the characters from her books. I talked about African Moses in *Mules and Men* and his wife Zipporah. "Zora and Zipporah. Zora and Zipporah," I chanted, loving the alliteration of their names. By this time, they were actual friends of mine.

I didn't sleep and continued showering repeatedly. I wasn't content to wash my hands over and over like Lady Macbeth. I snacked constantly to keep my strength up.

Ron came to assess the situation. Although he had previously seen me in the throes of mania, Jackie had not. Observing how much my behavior was scaring her, he escorted an overwhelmed Jackie out of the apartment. She returned later on Sunday and discovered I was gone. Nobody told her exactly what happened in her absence. By Monday, she figured out I wouldn't be back.

I told Cheryl I was engaged to marry someone from my church

who I definitely wasn't dating. By Saturday evening or early Sunday morning, Penny contacted Dr. Philippa Coughlin, the Director of Student Behavioral services. Dr. Coughlin arrived at my apartment to evaluate me. She conferred with my parents, using our house phone. Together, they agreed it would be best to get me back home. They wanted to avoid my being committed to Connecticut Valley Hospital for a second time.

Penny transferred the clothes I packed in Terry's garment bag to one of my suitcases. She, Cheryl, and I traveled by train from New Haven. A Wesleyan campus security guard drove us to the station. I experienced a glimmer of embarrassment with the brief intrusion of the rational thought, *This guard knows me.* A former Wesleyan student, he waited with us until we boarded safely. Returning to my reverie, I thought, *VIP treatment.* Throughout the trip, I was thinking how nice it was of my betrothed to send the three of us to Baltimore for spring break, early. Years later, Penny told me Wesleyan University purchased three tickets—round-trip tickets for her and Cheryl, and a one-way ticket for me.

CHAPTER TWENTY-ONE

Things Fall Apart

—TITLE OF A BOOK BY CHINUA ACHEBE

CHERYL, PENNY, AND I boarded the train in New Haven, CT for the six-hour Sunday ride to Baltimore. I sat in the aisle seat with Cheryl in the window seat next to me. Penny sat in the aisle seat directly across from me. Besides bathroom trips, I wasn't allowed to get up. If Cheryl got up to go to the café car or the bathroom, Penny sat next to me until she returned.

At one point, I asked Penny to buy me a mixed drink. She returned with orange juice and Sprite that she mixed together for me. Not allowed to go to the café car myself, I had to be satisfied with that.

I asked Cheryl, "Tell me again. Why don't you want me to have a conversation with these nice boys on the train?" I had spied a troupe of boy scouts who were travelling in our railway car. I was sure they would want to interact with me. Both of my friends instructed me to read my book. I removed my Shakespeare anthology from the Hello Kitty tote bag I had brought with me. I read a little, taking a break to color an eight-by-ten photo of myself with the green magic marker I had remembered to place in the bag. "I made the picture prettier," I enthused to my friends. I wanted to show it to the scouts, sure they would love it. Penny said no.

Finally, I fell asleep. Shortly after I awakened, we pulled into Baltimore's Pennsylvania Station. Penny carried my bag off the train. Cheryl walked close to me. *Why don't they have any luggage of their own*, I wondered. We took the escalator above ground to the station. A few feet from where we entered, I saw my mother and Uncle Vernon. That was nice of them to pick us up. I had figured we would catch a cab to my house like I usually did when I took the train home.

My uncle took my suitcase from Penny. Cheryl turned me over to my normally resolute mother, who now looked overwhelmed.

Penny and Cheryl each recounted later, separately, that although my mom knew each of them, from school as well as our home, she barely spoke to either of them as she whisked me away. Unable to concentrate on anything other than her sick child, my ultra-polite mother failed to thank them for their sacrifice. They returned to Connecticut on the next available train. According to her account, Cheryl was stunned by the experience.

My uncle drove my mother and me home. That night, my parents conversed into the night, formulating an action plan. I sat in another bedroom reading the biblical book *Song of Solomon*. I wanted to know what "but I found him whom my soul loveth: I held him, and would not let him go" meant. *Somehow, everything that was happening had to be connected to my upcoming nuptials*, I surmised.

The next evening my parents and I visited a psychotherapist in the Mt. Vernon area of Baltimore. Knowing a lot of artistic types resided there, I concluded, *He'll know what to do.*

The psychotherapist spent about twenty minutes talking to my parents and me before sharing his assessment of my condition. "Your daughter's mental health history suggests she suffers with the maturing form of bipolar disorder," he diagnosed. "Eventually she could require custodial care." He clarified his diagnosis, making sure my parents understood the unlikelihood of my finishing college. Marrying and having children were off the table.

He dismissed us with a book he had written in my hand. Back at home, I read through it, highlighting sections with my green marker and writing nonsensical notes in the margin. At the time, they seemed to me the illuminations of a genius.

When we left the doctor's office, I don't know why my parents did not take me directly to The Johns Hopkins Hospital for inpatient treatment. My mother knew it existed. Some years before,

Val, Karen, and I had visited my mom's first cousin Theodora at The JHH psychiatric unit on Christmas day. Like me, she was living with a bipolar diagnosis.

Denial is a powerful and sometimes dangerous thing.

That night, while my parents slept, I sat in the living room comparing photos of myself. *Did I look happier when I was thinner or heavier?* I chose heavier.

Then I decided to slip out of the house for a late-night walk. I walked two blocks from Finney Avenue to Greenspring Avenue, the main street. As I climbed up the hill, it magically became part of The Underground Railroad. I remembered Granny Ruth saying sometimes, when no one in her family knew where she was, she hid in plain sight, just like I was doing now. And then I was Billie Holliday, another Baltimorean. Carrying my Hello Kitty bag, my Shakespeare anthology, my green marker, some ribbons, and other miscellanea, I walked, songs from the movie *Lady Sings the Blues* reverberating in my head.

A gentleman saw me walking and offered me a ride. Without a thought about getting into a car with power locks driven by a stranger, I had him take me to the corner of Park Heights Avenue and Taney Road, less than a mile away. He said he was going in that direction. When we reached my destination, I got out of the car and noticed a City Paper box on the corner. The papers were free. I took one out and wrote some important messages on it with my green marker before returning it to the box. I removed a tiny stuffed bear from my bag and attached it to the box handle with a piece of ribbon I had been clever enough to bring. I needed to leave an Underground Railroad marker for the next traveler on my route.

I walked for a while thinking about my new task: establishing the new world order I had begun to outline in the back of my

Shakespeare anthology. Without planning to, I had reached Nome Avenue where Debbie W. lived. Granny Ruth always said, "God protects babes and fools."

Though surprised to see me, Debbie invited me into her familiar kitchen where I rattled on about this and that. Mrs. W. made me some tea before insisting she drive me back home. I accepted the ride, although I assured her I could have made it home by foot. When I let myself back in the house just before midnight, everyone was asleep.

The next day, my mother went to work. My father stayed home with me. I called a cab to go to noon-hour prayer with a group of mothers from my church, but my dad tipped the driver and sent him away after mentioning something about my "condition." Confused, I asked myself, *Does he think I'm pregnant?*

Later that day, I called another cab. Fortunately, it came while my dad was in the bathroom. I had the driver take me to Valerie's job at a bank in Towson. Never having been there before, I don't know how I was able to direct the driver to the branch. While the cabbie waited outside, I marched into my sister's office. She would know how to get our father off my back. "Val, Daddy's micromanaging me," came out in a whiny torrent. "I needed to get away from him, so I decided to visit, but only for a minute—my cab's waiting outside."

She looked at me directly and commanded, "Charita, wait here while I go talk to my manager." When she came back, she grabbed her purse, exhaled and announced, "I'm taking you back home." *Valerie is wise*, I figured, *that must be where we need to be next.* As we rode home, she seemed frustrated and a little angry. Thankfully, the anger didn't seem to be directed at me.

As my improvisational fervor increased over the next few days, my parents managed to keep me at home, giving me plenty of time to outline my new world order on the blank pages of my Shakespeare anthology. I also had time to read magazines. But, at the end of the week, I managed to elude my parents.

I walked five blocks and caught a bus downtown, compelled to attend happy hour at the Hyatt Regency Hotel. I never drink alcoholic beverages, but I ordered and drank a wine cooler. When it was time to pay, I didn't have any money. When I pretended I had left my money at home, a gentleman at the bar paid for my drink, no strings attached. When I tried to order another wine cooler, the bartender reminded me I had no money and politely asked me to leave.

When I refused, he summoned a member of the hotel security staff. I sat on the floor, refusing to move. "I'm staging a sit in!" I yelled. Soon, two Baltimore police officers arrived. Karen says my family was told I slapped one of the officers. I don't remember that, but I do remember an officer cuffing me before placing me in the back of the paddy wagon. One of the officers had to tighten the cuffs after I slipped my hand out of the cuff on my right wrist. At the station, they removed the cuffs and allowed me to do something I found exciting in the moment. They let me put my fingertips on a black inkpad and place my fingerprints on paper, like in kindergarten. I was glad I left my Hello Kitty bag at home. I might have gotten black ink on it.

That night, I stayed up all night in a cell singing, full voice. Some of the other women would yell out, "Shut up," from time to time. I guessed I wasn't singing the hymns they liked.

The next day was a Sunday. My mother, Valerie, and Karen came for a visit, as did my cousin Lela. I noticed they all looked worried. I told them about the tasty bologna sandwiches I had eaten and showed them the earring one of the women had given me that I had put through the piercing in my left ear. "It's a cannabis leaf," Karen noted disparagingly. "Take that out of your ear." After I did what she said, I lost my earring. My mother said something about an arraignment the next day. Val's brother-in-law, the attorney, would represent me. I tried to make sense of what they were saying.

Elder James Hickey, an apostolic minister from Baltimore, also visited me. He had received a master's in pastoral counseling from Loyola University, a Jesuit college that boasted one of the premier programs in the United States. He hoped to set up counseling sessions with me when I was released. Knowing of Elder Hickey's expertise, Bishop Geddis had put him in touch with my parents, hoping we could set up a beneficial therapeutic relationship.

My arraignment was held on Monday morning. My lawyer, noticing my wet linen jacket, grimaced, then asked, "How did your coat get wet? You didn't put it in the toilet, did you?" I had needed it to be wet so I could put it on to cool myself off. That small sink was not large enough for me to saturate it with water. I refused to answer his question.

CHAPTER TWENTY-TWO

"Herman Hesse called suicide a state of mind—and there are a great many people nominally alive, who have committed a suicide much worse than physical death: they have vacated life."
—JEANETTE WINTERSON

IN THE COURTROOM, my parents and my Baltimore pastor, Bishop B., stood with my lawyer and me as the judge heard my case. The judge's ruling included something about my need to be evaluated. That night, I woke up in a medication-induced fog at Springfield Hospital Center, the upgraded version of the Maryland State mental institution where my grandmother resided years earlier.

I had been committed again.

On March 15, 1982, Dr. M. Kim prepared an intake note which reads in part:

NAME COLE, Charita Lynette   CASE NO. 103278

Her memory, intelligence, orientation and abstraction capacity cannot be assessed. She has no insight, totally impaired judgement and excited and agitated mood and unpredictable behavior. She is quite angry and hostile.

PROVISIONAL DIAGNOSES:
Axis I: 296.40 Bipolar disorder, manic type
          295.70 Schizoaffective Disorder,
                 excited type
          295.20 Schizophrenia, catatonic,
                 excited

Axis II: 799.90 Diagnosis deferred on Axis II
Axis III: Deferred

ADMIT: Hitchman A-Wing

The following day, March 16, 1982, Dr. I. Turek provided the following Mental Status Examination, which is used to determine a patient's readiness for discharge.

In this interview Charita is observed to be tall, physically healthy, appearing her chronological age, female who was dressed properly. She, however, carried a posture which was markedly bizarre and facial expression which was quite grimacing, silly and inappropriate. Her motor behavior is observed to be moderately impared. She is pacing, restless, fidgety. Her general attitude was markedly uncooperative, moderately inappropriate. She had impaired functioning goal-directed activities. She was dramatic, sexually seductive. Her mood was markedly euphoric and hypomanic. Her affect was inappropriate in a moderate degree. Her speech was quite dramatic with an average rate and productivity. However, she was incoherent, irrelevant, evasive, with loosening associations. She was muttering at times in an unintelligent way. The content of thought could not be ascertained from her because she was so uncooperative. However, when she was left to spontaneous conversation, she stated the following: "Kelvin, stop those voices." She kept on screaming about Kelvin and Kelvin, she stated, was her brother. Then she continued on saying, "Do you know where Kelvin was born? Where is Kelvin? Are you Kelvin? I talked to him yesterday. Pluto is Elva's sister. Earth to Pluto, Earth to Pluto, Come in Elva, come in Elva. You don't

have to do that that way. This is a new City."
She then stood up and walked to the window and
looked outside and said, "Beautiful, this is really
Sykesville. I want to be in Brooklandville. Blue is
for hope, for Penny. My name is Gloria Penny. Penny
is my best friend. Gloria is my best friend. I need
Bill." All my efforts to get her to talk ratio-
nally were fruitless. She tried to seduce me; tried
to sit next to me. He wanted to read what I was
writing. She was laughing and having a good time.
She did not respond to the questions of delusions
or hallucinatory experiences.

Her orientation could not be tested. Her
cognitive functions seems to be disturbed. She had
marked degree of destructibility and marked degree
of attention disturbances. Her judgement was poor.
Insight nil.

PROVISIONAL DIAGNOSES:

Axis I: 296.44 Bipolar disorder, manic,
                with psychotic features

Axis II: V71.09 No diagnosis on Axis II

Axis III: Her previous laboratory
                   reports indicated Cushing's
                   Syndrome. Needs to be clari-
                   fied further.

This patient is mentally in need of impatient hospitalization. She will be a danger to her own
safety if she is discharged into her own custody.

This time, the doctors refused to let me come home if I did
not agree to be medicated with lithium. It took weeks for me to
benefit from it. I was also prescribed thorazine, a potent antipsy-
chotic that is now administered to patients in much smaller doses
than that prescribed to me. Internally, the combination of drugs
flattened my affect, making me feel like a zombie and bringing
back unwelcome memories of my childhood visit to see Granny
in Springfield.

As the psychotherapist predicted, each successive manic-depressive episode I experienced brought a higher high and a lower
low than its predecessors.

With prolonged use, lithium's most dangerous side effect is
kidney damage. When I discussed not wanting to take the risk
with Valerie, she assured me, with chief sibling assurance, "You'll
be all right." Adding humor, she continued, "If your kidneys fail,
you have six siblings. One of us is sure to be a match."

Karen visited daily. Since she is not a talkative person, she
encouraged me by showing up. Anytime I was ill, she dropped
whatever she was doing to do, what I labeled, asylum duty. Her
presence felt like she was sitting shivah for me, as is the Jewish
custom after someone dies. I was still in my body, but the life I
had embraced had ended. Most evenings, she brought my mother
with her.

Besides the first night of my commitment, my contact with my
father was solely by phone. I believe his experience in Connecticut

in 1980 when he could not prevent my CVH commitment had traumatized both of us. For the second time, he could not protect me from myself. His command that I rest my nerves was no longer enough to keep my mood balanced.

My mother brought a gentleman who had entertained a romantic interest in me to the institution in an attempt to cheer me up. As you might guess, the visit extinguished that spark. My dad had warned my mother that bringing him to visit me at a psych ward was a bad idea. I had no romantic interest in this suitor, but my mother saw his potential as a son-in-law. Yet I wondered, *Is this a bad omen?* If I was indeed broken, as in no longer smart—*would anyone ever want to marry me?*

Members of my church visited along with their children. A few years ago, I told my friend Jo Ann, "I was horrified when you brought your children to visit me at Springfield." I related the fear awakened in me when I visited my grandmother in an institution.

She laughed a little, then challenged, "Charita, name one child who was traumatized by those visits. We brought them because they loved you and asked to see you." *At least this Springfield upgrade smelled clean,* I concluded internally, after admitting the children suffered no harm.

At one point in my commitment, I was assigned a roommate who punched me in the jaw in a fit of rage that had nothing to do with me. A tech arrived in response to my shrieking and removed her from the room. She was assigned to another room where the staff could watch her more closely. This is the incident I remember most vividly from this nightmarish experience.

My Springfield Hospital Center Release Summary was submitted by M. Malayeri, M.D.

APRIL 16, 1982

22-year-old, black, single, female admitted to Springfield Hospital Center March 15, 1982
with two doctors certificates from Sinai hospital because she was excited, manicky, hallucinating auditorily, hearing voices from God, paranoid,
grandiose, delusional, unpredictable, and exhibited
some violent behavior.

When she was seen for Mental Status
Examination on March 17, 1982, she was found to be
grossly psychotic. She was angry, hostile, demand-
ing and abusive. She presented psychomotor agitation and she was unable to give proper account for
her admission. Most of the background information
was obtained from her mother [who] reported that
she had a previous psychiatric hospitalization
from December, 1980 until January, 1981. She was
hospitalized at Connecticut Valley State hospital
in Middletown, Connecticut for two weeks. She was
diagnosed as hypomanic. Apparently, since then she
had no outpatient therapy, except for the few times
she was seen at Sinai Outpatient Clinic and was not
given any medication. There was no history of using
drugs or alcohol in the past. On mental status
examination she was observed to be tall, physically
healthy, appearing her chronological age. She was
dressed properly. However, she carried a posture,
which was markedly bizarre and facial expression,
which was quite grimacing, silly, and inappropri-

ate. She presented psychomotor agitation. She was pacing, restless. Her general attitude was markedly uncooperative. She was grossly incoherent and irrelevant. Affect was inappropriate and she was mumbling at times in an unintelligent way. She had grandiose delusions with persecutory thoughts. Her impulse control was poor. Her behavior indicated having auditory hallucinations. She denies suicidal and homicidal thoughts. She was alert and oriented. Her insight and judgment were poor. Impression was Bipolar disorder, manic, with psychotic features. During this term of hospitalization, she received chemotherapy, milieu therapy and supportive therapy. She also participated in activity therapy. She was treated with the anti-psychotic drug; Thorazine. She gradually and slowly showed improvement. Psychomotor agitation, delusional thoughts, auditory hallucinations subsided. Since March 24, 1982, Lithium Carbonate was added to her treatment. She started home visit on 4-2-82, which was reported successful, and on 4-16-82 she was discharged to her family from home visit.

FINAL DIAGNOSIS:

Axis I: 296.44 Bipolar disorder, manic with
            psychotic features

CONDITION ON DISCHARGE: She was quiet and cooperative and she was free from psychotic symptomatology. She was considered to be in full remission.

PROGNOSIS: Short term prognosis is favorable. Long term prognosis considered to be guarded.

MEDICATION: Thorazine 100mg. a.m. and
200 mg. at bedtime
Lithium Carbonate 300 mg.
three times a day

AFTERCARE PLAN: Arrangement was made by social worker to be followed at Sinai Outpatient Clinic. (Psychiatric and Medical)

RESIDENCE: 4536 Finney Avenue,
Baltimore, Maryland, 21215

When I got home in April, my body felt heavy, like wet rags needing to be wrung out. Mentally, I felt like I was slogging through molasses, blindfolded. Meanwhile, I tried to forget the therapist's diagnosis of eventual custodial care, but it recurred in my thoughts, awakening a feeling of dread. My family did their best to cheer me. No longer on a manic high, I concluded, *I must be a real embarrassment to my family. I certainly embarrass myself.*

In May, I resumed my temp job in the accounts payable department at Johns Hopkins. Determined to avoid custodial care, I made my life as small as necessary, minimizing my innate theatricality whenever possible. In alignment with my erroneous assumption, I rehearsed, *my dramatic flair must be triggering these improvisational manias. I cannot serve both God and theater.*

I went to counseling sessions with Elder Hickey at The Abundant Life Counseling Center for a year. Mutually, we decided my therapeutic process had run its course. I placed myself squarely in an imaginary box with just enough space to sit, stand, lie down, and walk. Though breathing stagnant air, I was neither ready nor willing to explore the circumstances that controlled my thoughts. I would continue to pray and study my Bible, following the rules for living as taught in my Baltimore congregation.

I supposed, *nobody could have an episode living in this medicated stupor. Perhaps my present existence is as abundant as it will ever be.*

Still, I mourned my former life.

CHAPTER TWENTY-THREE

"I am terrified by this dark thing
That sleeps in me
All day, I feel its soft feathery turnings, its malignity"
—SYLVIA PLATH, "ELM"

THE LITHIUM THORAZINE mix was intended to normalize—read: dull—my moods. Thorazine was used to treat schizophrenia. The doctors were covering their bases.

It was hard for me to enjoy the new version of myself, yet I was coping. I went to work and church, including services in other states, but I really missed being energetic. I placated myself with the reminder, *the medications are working*. The therapist I saw each month at the Mt. Pleasant clinic agreed. I selected this hospital for psychiatric care because it was reputable and offered a sliding-scale fee. My temp job did not provide insurance. Although I hoped nobody would see me coming or going, I did not miss appointments.

Life continued. I vegetated in the accounts payable department at The Johns Hopkins University. Karen married her long-time boyfriend, John, in September 1983. I was a bridesmaid in the wedding. Teaching Sunday school provided a glimmer of joy.

On a Sunday in mid-October, I arrived at service late, having missed the Sunday school class, wearing a tabooed red silk blouse with my acceptable purple pencil skirt. During the morning message, the preacher spoke of taking burdens to the Lord and leaving them there. I decided I was healed of bipolar disorder and thought, *I'm taking my pills to the Lord and leaving them here*. At the end of the service, I knelt at the altar, placed my pills on its rail, and left them there. I informed my pastor I would not be needing the medication anymore and went home. After Mama called him, Bishop Byron brought the medication back to me the next day.

That week, I called out sick for two days. On the first day, I visited the recreation center around the corner and skated with the kids. I shared my imagined upcoming wedding with the center's director before leaving. On the second day, I visited a neighbor and shared my good news with her too. Completely out of character for me, I missed prayer service on Tuesday night. When Wednesday came, I missed my ride to work and rode public transportation to the Hopkins Homewood campus. I decided to get off the bus before my stop and walk three quarters of a mile to the campus, singing the song "Home" from *The Wiz*. I scampered along, sometimes singing in full voice, sometimes whispering, but always evoking the emotion of the song.

I stopped at an apartment building on my way to check on residents I did not know. No one was at home. I happened to have a religious tract in my purse, which I pushed under the door of one of the four units. When I got to my building, one of the women from human resources summoned the director of accounting services, a very kind man who took me into his office, having my supervisor join us. I vaguely remember being put into an ambulance, which took me to the emergency room at Union Memorial Hospital, at the intake department of Springfield State Hospital. Having no insurance, I was shipped to Springfield hospital once more.

How could I become manic while taking such a strong dose of medication? I had taken my medication as scheduled until I left the pills at church, at which point I was already cycling. I found my answer in a Yale University research study. Investigators discovered that some bipolar patients who suffered relapses while compliant to their medication routines experienced manias triggered by the feeling they were compelled to lead lives that ran counter to their inner desires.

As in 1982, one of the intake doctors thought I was schizophrenic rather than bipolar:

NAME COLE, Charita Lynette CASE NO. 106242

OCTOBER 11, 1983

This is a 23 year old, black female sent to Springfield Hospital Center with two physicians certificates citing: "Patient brought to Emergency Room by fellow employees at Johns Hopkins University because of unusual behavior. Patient has been employed at Hopkins since May, 1983 in accounts receivable.

At Springfield she is suspicious, she wants to read her paper then she stands up and yells "hallelujah" in a manicky manner. Although she has been diagnosed with bipolar disorder, patient gave impression that she is suffering from schizophrenia. She was given Haldol 5 mg. IM at sending emergency room; most of the time patient was sedated, unable to answer any further questioning.

PROVISIONAL DIAGNOSES:

Axis I: 295.20 Schizophrenia, catatonic, unspecified

Bipolar disorder/

This patient was received on Hitchman D-Ward.

I Esendal, M.D.

Some doctors, convinced that African-Americans are neither smart enough, nor creative enough to have bipolar, misdiagnose us with schizophrenia. This happened each time I was committed to Springfield. Fortunately, the doctor I saw the following day maintained the correct diagnosis of bipolar disorder, as the second doctor had in 1982.

SPRINGFIELD HOSPITAL CENTER
HISTORY SHEET

NAME COLE, Charita Lynette   CASE NO. 106242

OCTOBER 13, 1983

This is a 23 year old, black, single female who was admitted to Springfield Hospital Center on October 11, 1983 for the second time on two physicians certificates from Union Memorial Hospital. She was taken to the above hospital's emergency room by fellow employees at Johns Hopkins University because of unusual behavior. At the above hospital, she was described to be grandiose, delusional with flight of ideas, and showed elated mood and manic behavior. She could not sit still, singing, dancing, smiled inappropriately and was preoccupied with religiosity. According to her family, she was doing well until one week prior to

this admission when she stopped taking medication
and became restless. She has not slept or eaten in
the past two days. The patient has been previously
hospitalized at Connecticut Valley Hospital in
1980 and she was here in March, 1982. She has been
attending Sinai Outpatient Clinic and treated with
Lithium and Thorazine.

When the patient was seen on the ward, she
refused to relate herself and no full information
is obtainable at this time.

-J. Park, M.D.

SPRINGFIELD HOSPITAL CENTER
HISTORY SHEET

NAME COLE, Charita Lynette   CASE NO. 106242

OCTOBER 13, 1983

The patient is well groomed, colorfully
dressed, nice looking, young, black lady who
appears resistive upon approach by giving incoherent answers to the questions. She appears alert
and oriented, but her answers are unnecessary and
disconnected issues to the questions. She appeared
pleasant in her mood and her affect remained
elated and inappropriate. She was rather manipula-
tive and appeared to be dramatic in her behaviors.
She avoided direct questions by pacing around and

asking the name of each staff member, and no reliable information was obtainable from the patient. On gross observation, the patient appears bizarre in her behavior, smiling and laughing inappropriately, and appears to be preoccupied with her own thoughts. It was not whether the patient deliberately refused to answer questions or she was unable to engage in spontaneous conversation. Thought content cannot be tested, and no further interview is available at this time.

PROVISIONAL DIAGNOSES:

Axis I: 296.40 Bipolar Disorder, manic,
                unspecified.

TREATMENT PLAN:

Problem: 1. Elated behaviors of singing and
             dancing.
          2. Resistive to approach, refusing
             to answer questions.
          3. Poor compliance with outpatient
             treatment.

Treatment: 1. Haldol 5 mg. t.i.d. to reduce
               psychotic behaviors.
            2. Resume Lithium therapy.
            3. Milieu and activity therapies
               for inappropriate interaction
               with others.
            4. Individual counselling to
               recognize her need of treat-
               ment including medication.

NOTE FOR HEARING OFFICER:

The patient is stated to have become bizarre and manic after she stopped taking medication two weeks ago and she is unable to engage in coherent conversation at this time. She is elated and grandiose and behavior is grossly psychotic in hypermanic state. The patient suffers from mental disorder and requires further inpatient treatment until her condition further stabilizes for outpatient treatment. She is markedly impaired in her judgement due to manic behaviors and she will be a potential danger to her own welfare unless her condition stabilizes further.

-J. Park, M.D.

This commitment lasted longer than its predecessors. The doctors stopped the thorazine dosage and increased the lithium dosage. There was no behavioral counseling, just medicine lines in which I was given pills and juice under a nurse's scrutiny. Before I was to be released permanently, I had to travel home by bus to prove my independence. Karen drove me back from that humiliating experience I thought of as *flaunting my craziness on public transportation.* I saw someone I knew on the ride home; I'm glad he did not ask where I was coming from.

Sometime before Christmas, I slunk back to work. No one in the office mentioned the nature of my illness as they expressed their happiness over my return. The accounts payable department celebrated everyone's birthday simultaneously one day every

November. They sent me a birthday card, and when I returned, I received a raise.

At least once a week, someone would need to be present in the accounting services office during their weekly staff meeting. My supervisor assigned the task to me, giving me a break from microfilming during which time I meditated and read my Bible. The following May, I was hired to work in the Acquisitions Department at the Eisenhower library, the Homewood campus's central library. As a full-time employee, I received benefits, which included health insurance and an opportunity to take courses, free of charge. Using this perk, I completed the two courses needed to receive my degree: Hemingway In Our Time and Advanced Writing Seminar. I was awarded a degree from Wesleyan University in May 1985.

In the summer of 1985, I took a basic counseling course for which I was required to write a self-evaluation of my skills as a helper. My instructor and I found it very insightful. Introspectively, I identified my strong desire to control every situation that involved me. Part of the behavior grew out of my role in my family of origin; a greater part manifested from my attempts to avoid mania. I needed to relinquish the need to be in control of every situation. Rather than seek solutions for this shortcoming, I pulled the walls of my box closer to my body, leaving eyeholes for visibility.

CHAPTER TWENTY-FOUR

"Even the darkest night will end, and the sun shall always rise."

—VICTOR HUGO

BY THE END of 1986, I had been episode-free for three years. I was working in the Acquisitions Department at The Johns Hopkins University library. According to the Meyers-Briggs Personality Type Indicator, this job was a terrible fit for me. However, it was sufficient while I lived in the invisible box of my own creation. I inwardly repeated, *If I can keep myself small, the illness can't overtake me.* I took my medication, taught Sunday School, sang in the choir, performed motivational skits at church, and spent time with family and friends.

One Friday in early December, I noticed my thoughts were speeding up, accompanied by a gnawing, fearful sensation in my gut. For the first time, I recognized I was beginning to cycle. I spoke privately to my supervisor and our department head, Bev, in her office. When I revealed my bipolar diagnosis, Bev empathized with me. One of her close friends suffered with bipolar disorder. She asked what we needed to do. I decided to take a bus home where I would rest. One of my work friends took my bank card and withdrew money from my account so I could get home. I was unsure about what I would do next.

That Sunday, the Sunday School Department was in charge of the evening service. I was so tired that I spent much of the service in a room above the sanctuary. During his remarks at the end of the service, the pastor jovially commented on the ratio of single sisters to single brothers in the congregation—probably six to one, if not more. Then he added, "And Brother X. won't be single much longer." Oh Lord, the pastor had just provided one of the necessary elements for my improvisational manias. That brother was planning to be married, but, of course, I was not his fiancée.

The following day, when I called Brother X. on the phone to ask a question—after all, in my mind, we were about to be married—he wisely suggested I pose my question to my father. I hung up, forgetting the question.

I had spent the morning studying the latest issue of *Essence* magazine. As a teen, pre-salvation, I had expected to grace that cover one day. The model on December's cover was a young woman I knew from college. I took the magazine into the kitchen so my sister Ernestine could see this glowingly beautiful woman. After I finished gushing over the pictures, I relaxed in the living room, sipping the chamomile tea Ernestine made for me.

The next day, I went downtown and met a man who was selling beautiful leather bags at City Hall. I engaged him in scintillating conversation, which included my upcoming marriage to my imagined groom. Thinking and understanding through my hypomanic reverie, I convinced him I would be a profitable local distributor for his wares. After shaking hands on a business deal, I caught a cab home with ten handcrafted leather bags in my possession. I laid them out on my bed.

What did I do to deserve all of these beautiful bags? I asked myself. When Ernestine asked where I got all of those pocketbooks, I remembered some guy I met downtown had given them to me. I recalled he had said something about perceiving I was a "powerful woman." I told her she could have one. She looked at me skeptically. I told her I was going around the corner to visit my friend Sue. Maybe she'd want to come over and pick out a bag. When I returned a couple of hours later, my sister informed me I had just missed the bag designer. He rethought his decision to commission me as his merchandiser. Ernestine gave him all the purses, except the red leather bag I had taken to Sue's house. He was allowing me to keep that one. I now presume he figured out I was unstable after rethinking our interaction and decided he would be satisfied with recouping ninety percent of his loss.

That night, I walked to the apartments down the street to visit one of my sister's friends for the first time. In his absence, I invited myself in to chat with his sister. I don't remember how the visit devolved, but I ended up giving her a style lesson, changing in and out of the clothes in her closet. Taken aback by my behavior, she didn't stop me. She was relieved when I left for home.

The following evening, I felt like going shopping. I had one dollar. I stopped at St. Ambrose and borrowed enough money from Father Henry to buy an all-day bus pass. I boarded the bus and traveled to the Lexington Lady store in Mondawmin Mall. They sold lovely clothes in my size, fourteen. I had the greatest time in the store that evening. The sales women enjoyed my effervescence. We chatted as I tried on one outfit after another. When it was checkout time, I had spent nearly one thousand dollars on clothing and a necklace, although I never wore any jewelry beside broaches. I explained to the clerk that the money to cover the check had been placed in the account by my father, a wealthy businessman. I assured her it would clear that night. Accepting this fantasy as truth, she accepted my check with the proper identification.

I collected my bags and left the store as it closed. I waved goodbye to the sales clerk as warmly as I would if separating from a close friend. Then I used my bus pass to catch a bus downtown.

Having no money, I walked around downtown for a couple of hours. By this time, it must have been eleven at night. As I sat on a bench, a young man approached. He sat down and engaged me in conversation. By this time, I was becoming quite agitated, not knowing how I would get home. As we talked, I revealed my sister Linda worked at a downtown dance club, The Power Plant. The young man told me to turn around and look at the building behind the bench. It was the place where my sister was working. He instructed me to go inside and find her. I followed his directions as if he was the angel Gabriel and I was Mary, the mother of Jesus, while he rose from the bench and walked away.

Linda was shocked when she saw me at her job. Sanctified Charita never hung out at dance clubs. In my dancing euphoria, I grabbed and broke Linda's friend's necklace. Humiliated, as her friends called me crazy, Linda took me back to our Finney Avenue home. Very tired, I went to bed and immediately fell asleep.

The next morning, Dorothy Hurst, the sister from Calvary who my mother called my church mother, arrived at my house with a couple other concerned church sisters. Apparently, the night before, when no one was sure of my whereabouts, a contingent of family and church members had driven through the city looking for me. After I dressed, as Sister Hurst instructed, they drove me to the Mount Pleasant clinic.

For the previous three years, I kept monthly psychiatry appointments, had my blood tested at prescribed intervals, endured twenty-four hour urine collection and visited a therapist I didn't like. There was nothing particularly wrong with her; it was that I resented having to consult a therapist, period. And she never said anything I found meaningful. Then again, I never quite heard her because I was put off by what I perceived as a condescending manner. Bipolar or not, I found her tone intolerable.

When we arrived at the clinic, my friends explained my situation to the receptionist. We sat in the waiting area until my therapist called me into her office. Today, I chatted with her as I would with an old friend. "Your hair looks great! Have you done something different with it?" I asked, although it looked the same as always. Fortunately, Dorothy had accompanied me into her office to share the reality of my situation. After the doctor who was summoned spoke to me, the therapist informed us they were checking for an open bed on the psychiatric ward of the hospital. Finding no vacancies there, they found availability at Johns Hopkins Hospital at Wyman Park.

The therapist set up the transfer and my friends drove me to the psychiatric unit. Now that I had insurance, for the first time I was sent to a private hospital instead of a state facility.

My friends delivered me to the hospital safely, but were not allowed to remain with me. Later that day, my mom and Karen arrived to find a groggy, medicated Charita confined to a hospital room. I remember my mother commandeering my bankcard, checkbook, and ID. She asserted, "You won't be needing these." I thought, *I guess they don't trust me to be financially responsible. You write one bad check and they take your stuff.*

During this hospitalization, I had many visitors, including my family and friends from church. Because the hospital was across the street from JHU, where I worked, several of my friends and coworkers visited as well. One of my friends brought her pastor to pray with me. A coworker, a practicing Jehovah's Witness, discussed the Bible with me in what I saw as a good-hearted attempt to convert me. Overall, knowing people apart from my natural and church families knew about my condition was embarrassing.

My time at Wyman Park was more therapeutic than the state hospital stays had been, once I was medicated out of the mania. Clinicians discussed the illness and its prognosis with me. According to them, I should have been grateful for the three-year remission I had experienced...

To my surprise, for my birthday on December 15, the facility supplied a cake. I saved a piece for Brother X. Karen insisted, "He definitely won't be visiting" and ate the cake herself.

I was left with nearly one thousand dollars' worth of clothes, some worn, that I couldn't afford. When I shared my plight with my pastor, he formulated a plan. He, Dorothy, and I took the clothes back to Lexington Lady, where Dorothy was a frequent shopper. While I waited in the store, they went in the back to the manager's office and explained the shopping spree was a manifestation of bipolar mania. I felt humiliated by my out-of-control behavior, but was grateful that the store accepted every item purchased, leaving me with a zero balance. Thanks to my advocates' insistence, the manager even wrote off the lost necklace I failed to return.

Because my illness was arrested before developing into the full-blown manias of 1980, 1982, and 1983, the ensuing depression did not last as long as it had in those years.

When I was released from the hospital, Sister Hurst insisted we collaborate on a short play, *Is the Price Right?* for the church luncheon in April. Incidentally, by this time, the ban on attending plays had been lifted. She was sure writing a play would lift my spirits. "Even if you don't feel well enough to participate as an actress, writing the script will make you feel better," she assured me. By April, I had recovered sufficiently to act in the vehicle I created.

By the end of January, or early February, I returned to work, taking a medicinal dose of lithium that was slightly lower than the toxic dose.

CHAPTER TWENTY-FIVE

*"If you have a powerful gene, you get the illness no matter what—
it will come bursting through"*

—GLORIA HOCHMANN (*A BRILLIANT MADNESS*)

By 1986, I spent most Wednesday evenings with Aunt Nellie. She shared details of the Stanley family's intergenerational illness with me. Amazingly, she was not ashamed of her family's history of mania and depression. Though she had suffered bouts of despair, she had never suffered full-blown clinical depression.

My aunt wanted me to understand how my grandmother's illness affected my mother. She shared an incident that occurred while my mother was a teenager. During a manic episode, Granny Ruth disappeared from the residence she and my mother, her only child, shared, abandoning my mom. Mama hid my grandmother's absence for several days. When Aunt Nellie discovered her sister was gone, she brought her niece to live with her and her youngest sibling, Theodore, in the family home on Caroline Street. By this time, both of my great-grandparents were deceased. My mother never talked to her children about Granny Ruth's mental health history; I think it was too painful—and personally shameful—to discuss. As an adult, I mentioned inheriting bipolar disorder from the Stanley side of my family to my mom. She countered with, "Your father's sister was mentally ill." I corrected her, "Auntie was mentally challenged. That's not the same thing."

"Hmmph," she responded, shrugging her shoulders, thereby ending the conversation.

Because I was suffering the generational impact of the disease, Grandma Aunt Nellie—as I affectionately called her—thought it important for me to know how manic-depressive illness had affected the Stanleys. She told me how smart my grandmother had been, graduating from high school at age sixteen. My grandmother had told my older sisters and me she accelerated high school completion because she didn't like school, and dropping out was not a Stanley family option. Aunt Nellie remembered my grandmother's mania beginning as early as age seventeen. She also recalled my grandmother attracted "pretty" men. My maternal grandfather fit that category.

Other than my Great-Uncle Henry who suffered a head injury as a young child, my grandparents insisted the nine remaining children receive high school educations. Some pursued higher education. Great-Uncle Charles graduated from the school of music at Cornell University. Great-Uncle Theodore was a chemist who graduated from Morgan State University. This was an impressive family record for colored children raised in the early twentieth century.

Great-Uncle Edgar suffered from bipolar disorder as well. My sister Karen and I remember Uncle Edgar well. When he visited my mom, he always brought a half-gallon container of what we know and love as "cheap vanilla ice cream," our favorite. Aunt Nellie described him as a brilliant man whose jobs included being a normal school principal. In her words, "Edgar's life would fall apart and he'd have to put it back together again." His manias began around age twenty. At that time, there was no medication for those suffering with bipolar illness. The afflicted would be institutionalized until the doctors at the facility thought they were ready to go home. When my aunt was eighteen, she managed to care for her youngest brother, Theodore, as well as her mentally ill older siblings in the family home. My grandmother and Uncle Edgar were twenty-four and thirty-four, respectively. Their parents were deceased.

Aunt Nellie never expressed resentment over the challenges of caring for her family members, although she sacrificed her personal freedom and sometimes safety to do so. Uncle Edgar was known to bring random strangers into the house during his manic phases. She served her family, which included me. Given her experience as a caregiver, Aunt Nellie often reminded me,

"God blessed you. When your grandmother was sick, there was no medicine available to treat her. Your body responds positively to the medication that treats your illness." She also knew lithium treatments didn't work for everybody.

Thanks to my cousin James Stanley's genealogical research, I've come to understand how our family tree developed so many disease affected branches. In a phone conversation, he shared that he was able to trace our family back to 1705.

That year, Mary Stanley, a white woman, conceived a child with a black man through a consensual relationship. The Stanley family, a pocket of free blacks, intermarried and created their own community in Cambridge, Dorchester County, Maryland—the same Maryland County where Harriet Tubman, née Araminta Ross, was born on a plantation in 1822 and then escaped to freedom in Philadelphia, Pennsylvania in 1849. She was the famed conductor of the Underground Railroad, a secret network of places and routes created by abolitionists to safely transport slaves across the Maryland line to freedom in the northern bordering state of Pennsylvania. Tubman returned to Dorchester County more than one dozen times, alluding slave poachers and sheriffs.

By remaining in a tight-knit community, the Stanleys protected their status as free blacks. This desire to remain free forced them to intermarry, incubating certain strains of DNA. In our case, the Stanley descendants, including me, became more susceptible to clinical depression and bipolar disorder. Although this is akin to a generational curse, I owe my existence to their instinct for self-preservation.

In 2013, Dorchester County established the 11,000-acre Harriet Tubman Underground Railroad National Monument, part of the National Park Service. For easier accessibility to important sites from Harriet's time, the Park Service created the

Harriet Tubman Underground Railroad Byway, a driving tour that allows visitors to stop at significant landscapes related to that invisible railroad. Site number six on the tour, The Stanley Institute, was named in honor of my great-great-great-grandfather, Ezekiel Stanley. Hidden in the woods during the time of African-American enslavement, this one-room schoolhouse was moved, intact, to its present location in 1867—three years after slavery was abolished in Maryland.

Students were educated there until 1962. The school is listed in the National Register of Historic Places. I believe this is where my great-grandfather George, received his early education. This school is a testament to the community's determination to educate their offspring in a time when colored people were refused the privilege of learning to read and write.

Conducting my own research at the Enoch Pratt Library, I located information about my great-grandfather George Stanley, whose race was recorded as mulatto on the 1910 United States Census. Digging through old newspaper records, I found documentation naming him the first African-American to serve as a Maryland customs inspector. He also became the first African-American letter carrier in Baltimore. Shortly before marrying my great-grandmother Rosa King in 1895, he became an original stockholder and bookkeeper for The Lexington Savings Bank, an institution managed by prominent African-American men. *The Morning Herald* reported that the bank "was the only one of it's kind in Baltimore. It was supported entirely by colored people... [and] the institution catered entirely to the poorer classes." The business enterprise, lauded by Baltimore's Afro-American newspaper, folded in 1897 after a major scandal erupted surrounding the bank president's alleged embezzlement of its funds. The Afro included a sketch of my great-grandfather, a man who could have passed for white, if he had desired. Mama described him as a blue eyed red-head.

My great-aunt Polly passed first-hand information to her son, Jimmy. A close friend of Aunt Nellie's, she met and married my great-uncle George Stanley Jr. According to Jimmy, Granny Ruth's sibling group was stigmatized and taunted openly. Although Aunt Polly didn't share specific descriptions of the family's behavior, Jimmy recounted his mother's memory of neighbors calling my grandmother and her siblings the Crazy Stanleys.

I have endured being called crazy at different times in my life. I understand witnesses to my off-kilter behavior lacked the understanding and language necessary to process what they were seeing. With limited understanding, they reached conclusions similar to those I formulated as a nine-year-old child after my visit to Springfield State Hospital.

Now that I have achieved a largely asymptomatic, even mood, people who know nothing about my mental health history sometimes speak quite pejoratively in my presence about those who suffer with bipolar disorder. Some people expect those suffering with bipolar disorder to swing from chandeliers and exhibit all manner of outrageous behavior, continually. I have remained silent, never attempting to correct their unlearned notions.

I now understand the truest motivation for my silence. I did not want anyone who had no idea to know I was one of the crazies of whom they spoke.

CHAPTER TWENTY-SIX

"Don't defy the diagnosis, try to defy the verdict."
—NORMAN COUSINS

MY LIFE HAD unraveled so much. I was uncertain about my secular future as well as my Christian identity. Having denied the psychotherapist's diagnosis of maturing bipolar disorder for so long, I finally acknowledged its accuracy. Then, I reasoned, *If I internalize and implement effective strategies, I know the God I discovered in first grade will help me to enhance the quality of my life.*

After being released from Wyman Park's psychiatric unit, I contacted Elder Hickey and updated him regarding my recent psychiatric hospitalization. I almost begged him to resume the therapeutic process at Abundant Life Counseling Center where the driving principle was People Growing Toward Wholeness. When he agreed to pair his therapeutic acumen with my determination, somewhere in my spirit, I knew I would recover. I still had to convince my mind and my heart.

Returning for a second round of therapy, I was determined to destroy anything in my psyche that blocked my progress. If I could, I wanted to decrease the frequency and severity of my cycling. I had been episode-free for three years before I returned to this bottom. I had taken my medication as prescribed, had regular blood tests, and endured yearly extended urinalyses. And, of course, I had remained in my box.

The center now required clients' medication management to be overseen by the staff psychiatrist, Dr. Smith. I agreed, knowing Elder Hickey's pastoral care would excel any treatment the clinic had provided. I could say goodbye to the therapist whose tone I despised. Although I was resistant to therapy in 1983, I had learned Jim Hickey possessed the therapeutic capacity to see my potential and reflect confidence back to me. As he used this skill effectively, with my agreement to actively participate in the wellness process, my mental health was sure to improve.

Every Tuesday for more than two years, unless one of us was

on vacation, Jim Hickey and I met, discussing topics I chose. Early on, we had to discuss the self-perceived negative impact I—that is, my illness—had placed on the Cole family.

Rather than impacting the world, as I had predicted in my senior essay before leaving Park, I worked in the acquisitions department at the JHU library. Not a menial job, but not what I felt called to do. My brother Martin once declared with disdain, "We wasted our money sending you to that school," speaking of Wesleyan University. I retorted, "I don't remember receiving any checks with your name on them while I was at school." Although I had a comeback line, his statement reinforced my opinion that I had morphed from family academic superstar to family failure. And I really hadn't drained my family financially. I had strained it emotionally.

I had developed an ugly duckling mindset concerning my role in the Cole family. Though it seems melodramatic to me now, while viewing myself through my periscope of hypersensitivity, I decided I was the defective sibling. Some days, deep within myself, I shouted, *Do you think I like being crazy?* During the therapeutic process, I learned to accept and love less than perfect me.

My emotional intelligence quotient needed a boost. Living in my box and wanting to avoid severe mood swings from elation to despair, I had locked myself into an unbalanced and unrealistically happy mood. Sadness, frustration, and anger became taboo emotions. It was important for me to learn how to regulate my feelings and my moods. I had to identify the emotions I had hidden under my salvation cloak of happy, happy joy. The most notable were fear, guilt, shame, and condemnation.

During my sessions with Elder Hickey I considered real-life scenarios, using a technique similar to theatrical scene study, whereby I forced myself to develop greater self-awareness. I acknowledged how positively my mother's faith had impacted me. As Lena Younger told her daughter Beneatha in *A Raisin in the Sun*, "In my mother's house, there is still God."

Formalized Catholicism had provided a foundation for victorious living. Now understanding the Old Testament prohibition against praying to graven images, I no longer accessed God through dead saints. I now prayed to God through Jesus. Being a pastoral counselor, Jim Hickey opened and closed each of our sessions with prayer.

For a short time, he had me join a therapy group. I discontinued the process. I needed to focus my energies on regulating my own emotional health rather than entertaining and being drained by the spirit of depression that enveloped the group.

In one session, Elder Hickey asked me, "Charita, what do you really want to do?" Without hesitation, I replied, "I'd like to establish a Christian arts collective for youth. Besides studying vocal and instrumental music, they'd learn dance, drama with improvisation, and visual arts." "Why haven't you pursued that vision?" he asked. I had been living such a myopic Pentecostal lifestyle for so long, I no longer thought it was possible. Being an Apostolic pastor, Jim Hickey informed me that Pentecostal churches did exist in which members were encouraged to immerse themselves in the arts. "An abundant life includes more than eating, sleeping, going to work, going to church, and going home," he declared. Since I'd received the Spirit of God in 1979, no preacher in the holiness churches I'd belonged to had embraced this opinion.

In more recent years, many congregations have updated their views concerning arts accessibility for born-again believers. Perhaps someday I will become involved in theater again. I would love to direct a play.

I had to explore my feelings about my parents' marriage. I

discovered I was angry with my mother for being *too submissive* to my dad. Although he provided financially, I felt nobody should endure emotional abuse. Though they were both part of the cycle, my reaction to what I had seen was a personal refusal to take crap from any man. As we explored my feelings, I was able to understand how unreasonable my expectations of my mother had been. Here was a woman, raised by an actively bipolar mother, who managed to keep her own family together. She was not going to abandon her children, nor did she expect us to abandon one another. I released the anger, realizing that Mama loved my siblings and me and made decisions concerning our well-being based on her personal evolution at any given time.

My Mama is an amazing woman.

I ACKNOWLEDGED MY parents' love for me and accepted their interactions as unique to their relationship. I decided individual couples set the parameters for their relationships. A few years ago, I summoned enough courage to ask my elderly mother, "Why didn't you leave Daddy?" She replied, "I had seven children." I now understand that she, like my father, was committed to their marital relationship.

Because Elder Hickey was a pastoral counselor, we applied Biblical principles in my recovery process. He encouraged me to move beyond mental assent—knowing in my head that a scripture is true—to faith, personally applying the scriptures I read. In addition to traditional clinical conversational practices, he encouraged me to memorize specific scriptures, especially those that counterbalanced the fear I internalized and embraced in response to bipolar illness. I came to understand that I didn't fear failure. I feared success. Finally realizing why I lived in a self-constructed box, I asked myself, *do I possess the temerity to step out of my box?*

By 1988, I formed a visual description of whom I had become: a faceless little girl in a yellow dress who had consigned herself to the west wing. In reality, the whole mansion and property belonged to her. For me, yellow was the color that symbolized hope. Even though my face was indistinct, it wasn't distorted like the face of Merrick, the elephant man. I decided to embrace strength and move forward. Though it sounds trite, I had to figure out who I really was.

I noticed I had changed over the course of my illness. My former haughtiness had been replaced by humility and compassion. I figured nobody could exhibit the levels of out-of-control public mania I did and remain arrogant. Now, my interpersonal skills were even stronger than they had been in my Arts Circus days. Emotionally, I was developing both social expressiveness and social control.

It was most difficult for me to explore the shame I felt in the depressive phase of each episode, especially regarding the fiancé theme. I worked through a lot of psychic pain to ready myself for a loving relationship. As an eye-witness to my parents' in-fighting, I had grown reluctant to surrender control in a relationship. No man was going to boss me around. I finally understood what a young man in my college class was seeing in me in 1977 when he asserted, "Charita, you intimidate guys." I learned to allow myself to appear more vulnerable.

Toward the end of the therapeutic process, the unboxed me was forced to discover I was not as open to having a husband in real life as my delusional reveries suggested.

CHAPTER TWENTY-SEVEN

*"I have the nerve to walk my own way, however hard,
in my search for reality, rather than climb upon
the rattling wagon of wishful illusions."*
—ZORA NEALE HURSTON

OSCAR WILLIAM BROWN, Jr., a minister I knew from church, called me for the first time in September of 1988. He had been thinking of me. "The best way to get someone out of your head is to talk to them" he insisted.

I had known Oscar for many years. We were part of a four-church fellowship that met quarterly, the Apostolic Festival—comprised of churches from Baltimore; Washington D.C.; Philadelphia; and Penns Grove, New Jersey. As members of the New Jersey congregation, Oscar directed the choir for those services while his wife Mary played the piano. She died of breast cancer complications in 1985, having declined medical intervention. Oscar's sister Gloria and I were present at his parents' home in Delaware the night he came home from claiming her body from a hospital in New Jersey. Mary passed away while visiting her sister, who insisted she go to the emergency room. The couple had moved in with his parents while she was ill.

One of the more ebullient people I have known, Oscar entered the room deflated by grief. The four family members assembled in the room asked him how he was doing with no displays of physical affection. Belonging to a family that embraced in times of grief, I wanted to hug him, but decided against it. Having spent several hours in the Browns' home while waiting for Oscar, I noticed how emotionally detached they seemed from one another. I didn't want to violate their cultural boundaries.

We talked for over an hour about various topics. He remembered the birthday card I sent to cheer him up the year after his wife died. He had kept that card since 1986. During our initial phone conversation, I informed Oscar I had deferred admission to the Masters in Library Science program at Simmons College in Boston, Massachusetts. Having deferred my admission for a year,

I would matriculate in September 1989. I didn't share why I had decided to defer.

After hanging up the phone, Oscar later said, he thought, *Lord, she's moving to Boston*, and laid on his bed to ponder that glitch in his plan.

After our phone conversation, I didn't speak to Oscar again until November. Meanwhile, I had changed my mind about attendance at Simmons. Given the distance from Baltimore to Boston, I questioned my ability to stay healthy so far away from my supportive family. Oscar and I reconnected at a birthday party for one of his closest friends. I attended the birthday bash, in spite of a cold, because I expected to see Oscar there.

When I saw Oscar, I told him I had changed my mind about graduate school without sharing my rationale regarding the change. He gave me his number and asked me to call. I did wait a day.

AFTER CONTACTING OSCAR, I told Jo Ann about Oscar's call in September, asking if she thought he had a romantic interest in me, as I suspected. Jo laughed and said, "No man calls a woman and talks for an hour just to talk. Women do that." Oscar later confirmed her statement, informing me, "I'm not looking for a friend. I already have female friends."

Oscar pursued me, something I had grown unaccustomed to while battling bipolar disorder. By my birthday on December fifteenth, we had gone out three times, spoken by phone daily, and corresponded by mail. For my twenty-eighth birthday present, I received a marriage proposal. According to Oscar, our union was *inevitable*. He likened himself to the man in the Biblical parable who, finding the treasure in the field, sold all he had to buy the field, thereby obtaining the treasure. Knowing I might minimize the significance of this analogy, he assured me, "You are the treasure."

Years later, a friend teased me about how quickly I had agreed to marry Oscar. When I shared this anecdote, she exclaimed, "No wonder you married him! I would have married him too."

Motivated by Oscar's unconditional positive regard, I shared the unboxed me. I had rediscovered I could live healthily outside the fortress I had created around myself. That was the woman I allowed Oscar Brown to get to know. On our second date, I read him poetry from *for colored girls*. One Saturday night, we attended a puppetry show at Theatre Project. I was delighted to see Philip Arnoult, who remembered me as one of the *theater kids*.

Of course it was essential that Oscar understand my illness. I invited him to a therapy session in which Elder Hickey could help me explain bipolar disorder coherently. After our discussion, Elder Hickey gave Oscar literature that described what was known at that time about this brain-based disease. The only other person I had invited to a therapy session had been Karen. I wanted to silence her insistence that I was doing better because of medication alone.

With some understanding of bipolar disorder, Karen suggested I wait until Oscar and I were married to reveal my bipolar diagnosis. I informed her, "He already knows." Then I asked, "Don't you think it would be unfair to hide something that major from somebody who's promising to stay with me for the rest of my life?" She didn't seem convinced my decision was best.

The Tuesday night Oscar returned home after our meeting with Jim Hickey, his mother asked, "Did you know Charita spent time in a mental hospital?" Having been members of the same church, Oscar's sister, Gloria knew about at least one of my hospitalizations and had shared my mental health history with their mother. My fiancé was relieved to be able to share information about bipolar disorder with her, but in truth, the mental institution part hadn't crossed his mind.

Oscar was the pastor of the remnant of the Church of the Lord Jesus Christ his father had shepherded until his death from cardiac arrest in December 1986. I suggested he convene a meeting in Delaware to discuss my illness with the fundamentalist Christian members of his family as well as his congregation. Many of them thought mental illness wouldn't affect *faith believers*, as they called themselves. At that time, and even today, some Pentecostal believers erroneously attributed mental illness to demon possession. Oscar nixed my idea. Adamantly opposed, he declared, "We don't need to have a meeting. In comparison to the members of the congregation, you are as spiritual as any of them if not more so."

The devoutly Apostolic members of Oscar's family tried to convince him to not marry me. Interestingly enough, one of the naysayers was Oscar's grandmother. I had visited her several times with Gloria. On one occasion, unaware of my bipolar diagnosis, she told me I was "a wonderful example of a young, saved sister." When he continued to date me, some family members told him outright that God was against our union.

Oscar did pose a question to me that I pondered, finding it reasonable. "Would you want someone in your family to marry someone with your illness?" Without answering, I thought, *if they have the faith they claim, shouldn't it conquer any disease?* The real issue was that they viewed mental illness as demonic possession, not as an illness.

Oscar tried to convince me it didn't matter what his family thought about our relationship. "After all," he insisted, "you're marrying me, not them. After our marriage, I understood why Oscar refused to green-light that meeting. He knew if I had met with his people, it was likely their attitudes toward me would have changed my mind about joining his family and congregation. Exposing me to his them was a risk he was unwilling to take.

Since Mary's death, I was the third woman Oscar had courted. One of the women he pursued was not a fit due to scriptural differences. The other decided the relationship wasn't right for her. Our relationship was both loving and harmonious. Oscar shared that his wife Mary, having interacted with me at church, once mentioned, "Sister Charita is going to make someone a good wife." Since this affirmation predated her illness, Mary's words counted as a vote in my favor.

Although I wanted Oscar's circle to embrace our union, it was not the issue I stumbled over. When my close friends inquired about my relationship with Oscar, I described it as warm, relaxing, and pleasant. When we were together, my heart didn't race, my hands didn't shake, and there were no knots in my stomach. Good news. I wasn't afraid of him. But with a proposal in play, I was forced to acknowledge my truth: marriage *terrified* me.

I loved Oscar deeply, and the sincerity of his love had erased my fear of being dumped, that had taken root after my relationship with Jerry ended. Still, I wasn't sure I could marry *anybody*. I asked him, "What if our relationship mirrors my parents' marriage, happy for a few years before becoming an emotional battle royal?"

Oscar shared his feelings, brought on by my hesitancy about being married.

In this letter dated February 24, 1989, he wrote:

Dearest Charita:

I think of how much I have come to love you, and I am delighted to know this love. To have had a glimpse of who and what you are only increases my desire to love you more. It is heartwarming to know that it is received and returned with equal fervor.

As we labor to overcome our inadequacies, know above all else that I love you dearly. As long as we keep sight of our love for each other, we will pull together and not apart. Any urge to pull away would be dangerous for us. Real safety lies in the center of love not on its fringes. I ask you to try to understand my reaction when my heart perceives a pulling from the center.

While on your part, in your attempt to deal with these pulls, this is a necessary process. My first reaction is that I try to deal with thoughts of you trying to get away from me. A flood of thought comes to bear all at once saying:

A) Stupid, can't you see that she is trying to tell you without really telling you that she doesn't want to do this.

B) How long will it take to get through your thick head that maybe she'd rather not love you, for whatever reason.

C) If she really loved you, she wouldn't be going through this. After all, you're not.

So while you are addressing your concerns, they bring out concerns in me. As we struggle to overcome, let us be considerate of each other's dilemma.

Love you, Oscar

Oscar included a poem he wrote for me with that letter.

Your Love

I want your love to have and to hold
To love you with every fiber of my being is my goal

To see our love excel each preceding day in tenderness and strength
To cultivate it, to motivate it, to stimulate it I'd go to any length

To manifest it, to testify of it with the uttermost glee

Rest assured, my love, your love is cherished by me

To feel the power and flow of your love excites me beyond measure

I liken it unto the man who found the field of great treasure

When I think of the joy of having your love all my life long

It causes my soul to rejoice and my heart to break forth in song

My Love Always

Oscar

2-24-89

While Oscar and I continued our daily communication, I confronted the roots of my feelings to decide whether or not I possessed the desire and the strength of character required to be someone's wife. I concluded, my mind, will, and emotions were more than stable enough for me to commit to marriage to Oscar Brown, Jr.

On March 9, 1989, I wrote:

Oscar Brown,

Years ago, some poor misguided souls sang a song about "a love that bears no strings . . . a love that touches, but never clings." Back then, such a concept sounded pretty nice. (I was young then.) In more recent times, I abandoned non-cling love for an all-encompassing, life-altering love. The Lord knew what I wanted and needed; he sent me the desire of my heart: Oscar William Brown, Jr.

To my surprise (or was I surprised?), your love scared me. And that story you had to live through with me. But, I believe the tumult has ceased. I knew I'd be alright if I pressed my way through the shaking. Thank you for pressing through with me and assuring me your love is and always will be a constant in my life. I am amazed by the level of love you show me as well as its superlative quality.

I am convinced that you are the man I want to commit myself to as long as we both shall live. Fortunately, you plan to pledge yourself to me as well. Behind closed doors, alone together, we can abandon any false fronts we show others and relax into one another. I marvel that I feel so comfortable with you.

You may never know how much I praise God for sending you my way. We came together in the fullness of time. Spending the rest of my life completing your life with my love looks better and better to me as June 10 approaches.

I promise you all the love you need as you need it . . . it's what you deserve in return for the eternal love you've given me and the well-spring of love you've awakened in me.

My love is yours forever,

Charita

I included a heartfelt companion poem with my letter—not to be outdone.

For Oscar Brown, Jr.—1989

i had almost convinced myself
that the good things in life
were too good for me
i could see them
i kept them at a distance
slightly beyond my grasp

then one day . . . you touched me

i couldn't convince you to leave—
i attempted my usual method
let him think
i'm really not interested
he'll find a way out on his own
and I escape commitment once more

but you refused to let me go that easily

thank you for hanging in there
for weeding through the mixed signals
and the idiosyncrasies
to discover
the untapped wellspring of love
that lay dormant
waiting for someone to activate it gently
and nourish its free flow

—Charita L. Cole

I had a wedding to plan. That Saturday, Valerie and I went to Sonia's Bridal where I purchased my wedding gown.

CHAPTER TWENTY-EIGHT

"Faith is
...Ceasing to worry, leaving the
FUTURE
To the God who controls the future."
—PAMELA REEVE

I DESIGNED OUR carefully worded wedding invitation with Oscar's feedback. Printed with black italicized script on pale pink parchment paper, it read, in part,

> *Knowing we have chosen*
> *God's will for our lives*
> *Charita Lynette Cole*
> *And*
> *Oscar William Brown, Jr.*
> *together with our parents*
> *Mr. and Mrs. Leonard Cole*
> *and Mrs. Anna V. Brown*
> *invite you to share in our joy*
> *as we pledge our lives to each other*
> *before the Lord Jesus Christ*

Mama, Val, Karen, and I mailed out invitations to most of the guests on Oscar's and my lists. Oscar hand-delivered invitations to his family and congregants. I hand-delivered invitations to the adult members of my small church as well, to avoid exclusions. During our pre-marital counseling sessions, my pastor and his wife told us they were sure the congregation would look forward to celebrating with us. I was the founder of the Children's Ministry, and Oscar was a ministerial favorite.

During our courtship, Oscar attended many services at Calvary, prayed with individual saints and preached on several occasions. He also directed the choir for our anniversary service in May.

Joining two lives, Oscar and I had to discuss and negotiate belief systems. Like traditional Catholics, Oscar did not believe in the use of birth control. Members of his church married without wedding rings as did the members of Calvary Church in Baltimore. I was willing to follow those teachings, with plans to wear Oscar down until he bought me a ring. There was no scriptural support for the no-jewelry clause to which he adhered. Penny bought me a plastic ring that I kept, reminding me of the band which was to come.

As part of his commitment of his body to God, Oscar did not go to doctors. His belief in faith healing had taken root as a teenager when his younger brother accidently shot him in the leg while hunting. Oscar's father—and Bible teacher—was willing to take him to the hospital to have the bullet removed, but he decided against medical intervention. He chose to walk in faith, leaving the bullet in his leg and suffered no complications. When I looked at his calf, there was an entry wound, but no exit wound.

Unlike many members of Church of the Lord Jesus Christ at that time, Oscar had decided going to a doctor is a personal decision. He shared with me that when Mary's condition was worsening, he encouraged her to see a doctor, but she decided against it. As for me, I took medication to offset the biochemical imbalance in my brain. Continuing to take lithium was non-negotiable. Oscar agreed I should follow the regimen that was keeping me healthy.

Three weeks before our wedding, I met with my psychiatrist to get a new prescription and to discuss pregnancy risks for women taking lithium. He informed me that lithium could damage a baby's heart during the first trimester of pregnancy. If I became pregnant I would have to suspend lithium use under psychiatric supervision.

I shared my doctor's assessment with Oscar. The thought of going off medication frightened me. Plus, Oscar did not sanction the use of birth control under any circumstances. He believed his strong faith and love would sustain us through a pregnancy. He promised, "I'll be your medicine."

Unsure as to whether or not I would go through with the marriage, I decided to pray. I remembered God had directed me to forego my trip to Paris in 1979 where I would have suffered my first significant hypomanic episode.

I explained my dilemma to Elder Hickey, Jo Ann and my pre-marital counselors, asking for prayerful support rather than advice.

Convinced in my spirit that I could suspend lithium use for a short time during pregnancy, I let Oscar know we would go through with the marriage.

Elder Hickey and I had our final therapy session at the end of May. Believing my union with Oscar would be mutually beneficial, he agreed to deliver the prayer of Invocation at our wedding. Elder Hickey noted that I had gone through this cycle of therapy without transference or regression, which he considered an unusual feat. Many people who enter therapy rely on their therapist as a savior and improve in a peaks and valleys projection. I already had a God and was so determined to get well that I improved without plateauing.

We reviewed the growth areas I had been most resistant to in February 1987:

1) Moving and acting on faith
2) Confrontation with authority figures, primarily my dad, and
3) Committed non-platonic relationships.

I was now doing well in each category. Additionally, I had rid myself of the torment that accompanies the fear of relapse. I accepted the Biblical truth that rather than the spirit of fear, God had given me a sound mind. I would take my medicine, pray, and keep my stress levels down. In situations where emotions flared, I'd have to keep calm or walk away.

My counselor and I revisited my tendency to want to think of myself as less than others because of my illness. I had to remind myself that as a human being, I was no better or worse than anybody else.

Before our final prayer together, Elder Hickey first praised me for the courage I displayed in destroying my box, then reminded me I was marrying a man who understood love and knew how to express it. He reminded me I had said, "This relationship is what I deserve." Establishing eye contact with me, my insightful therapist advised, "Trust Oscar, and talk to him non-defensively."

On Saturday, June 3, 1989, we rehearsed for the wedding. Although we didn't repeat the vows, we listened as the pastor read them aloud. I was terrified. After the rehearsal, I approached my pastor, wide-eyed, babbling about my inability to commit to a marriage. He smiled and stated, "You're marrying Oscar next week."

Karen hosted a luncheon for the bridal party and our parents after the rehearsal. I distributed gifts and thanked the members of the bridal party for their love and support. After Oscar and I were alone, I had a problem to address with him concerning his mother. She absented herself from the day's activities. When I asked, "Honey, where's your mother?" He told me she wasn't coming. Not only had she missed the rehearsal, she was not planning to attend our wedding. I was livid. When I spent Memorial Day weekend at her home, she was very nice to me, as usual, never giving any indication of her true feelings concerning my marriage to her son.

My initial thought was, *What is wrong with her? Even his first wife's sister approves of this union and of me.* I took a moment to reign in my emotions, but still blurted out, "If she doesn't come, she will never have access to any child I have." Recognizing this as an over-the-top reaction, I conceded to Oscar I wouldn't do that. Then I lashed into him.

"Why did you let me put your mother's name on our wedding invitations, knowing she was opposed to our union. Now our invitation is tainted by a lie." To calm me down, Oscar explained he had been certain he could convince his mother to attend. He had been wrong. In an attempt to appease me, he shared his mother's belief that "you really love me." Oscar's sister Gloria was the sole member of his immediate family or congregation who was present for the ceremony.

Mother Brown later told me she felt the timing was not right for Oscar to marry. No animosity was directed at me, "You were caught in the crossfire." To which I replied, "If you die in the crossfire, are you any less dead?" In time, with mutual effort, we were able to develop a loving rapport, as evidenced by the absence of knots in my stomach when we spent time together.

This family's reaction underscored how misunderstood mental illness is for the general population. It seems to hold an even greater stigma among African-Americans and fundamentalist Christians. My victory was being able to withstand opposition without feeling like a lesser person. I was going to claim my gift from God: Oscar William Brown, Jr.

CHAPTER TWENTY-NINE

"To have and to hold from this day forward..."
—TRADITIONAL CHRISTIAN WEDDING VOW

BEFORE OUR WEDDING day, Oscar promised to love me more than any individual person could. I believed in that love. When he remained in our relationship, against the advice of most of his family, I knew Oscar Brown, Jr. was committed to building a life with me.

Our marriage ceremony was attended by my loyal supporters. My sisters served as bridesmaids. My closest friends sat at the front of the church, wearing corsages along with Mama and Aunt Nellie. My father escorted me down the center aisle of the church to the altar where Oscar was waiting. My brothers, Uncle Vernon, my cousin Lela and Marion Dixon were present as well. Looking at my support team, I was reminded that their love had carried me through precarious times.

Although manias mortified me, while I scampered through them, I was having a splendid time. At those times my team protected me from myself. They further protected me when I was despondent, standing in the gap between me and suicidal thoughts through their prayers, presence, and faith.

Like others given bipolar diagnoses, I had days when I thought, *what's the use?* Those were the days when I felt like the molasses I slogged through was sure to suffocate me. Then, amidst all the turmoil that had become my life, I learned to surround myself with love—from God and the people who cared enough about me to cheer me through to triumph.

am grateful my parents taught my sibling group how to function as a unit when we were children.

AFTERWORD

"Those who do not have power over the story that dominates their lives, the power to retell it, rethink it, deconstruct it, joke about it and change it as times change are truly powerless because they cannot think new thoughts."
—SALMAN RUSHDIE

ON NOVEMBER 20, 1991, my husband Oscar William Brown, Jr. died at age 40. We had been married two and a half years and were parenting nineteen-month-old Liana and six-month-old Anita. I felt abandoned for the first time.

A month after the funeral, the girls and I moved to my childhood home on Finney Avenue at my parents' insistence. My family and closest friends feared I might be facing an insurmountable stressor and braced for the relapse, which never occurred.

After a year spent trapped in an emotional haze of grief, I forced myself to assess my condition. I concluded, *Oscar is dead, not me*. Then I prayerfully devised a plan. The girls and I moved into our own home near my parents. I earned an accelerated master's degree in early childhood education and found employment as a teacher.

I have raised the girls with support from my Cole and Brown families and close friends. Liana earned a bachelor's degree in 2012. Anita is progressing toward her bachelor's degree.

The Cole siblings have designed an assisted living system that will allow our elderly parents to remain in their own home as long as possible. I serve as care manager for our endeavor.

Having reassessed my life, I discovered I am not the failure I thought I might become after hearing the death knell in that therapist's office in 1982.

I defied the verdict.

Acknowledgments

Besides my family of origin, I have been blessed to parent two phenomenally supportive women, Liana and Anita Brown. I also appreciate the in-laws, aunts, nieces, nephews, and cousins who have encouraged me to tell my story.

I am grateful that When Words Count Retreat exists in Vermont. Steven and Neile Eisner provided much-needed encouragement as I completed the book and went on to win the retreat's Book Deal competition. The prize was this book's publication. I appreciate the judges, Marilyn Atlas, Ben Tanzer, Meryl Moss and Catherine Marenghi and send love to my fellow contestants from Pitch Week V.

I appreciate my publisher at Curbside Splendor Publishing, competition judge Victor D. Giron. I was fortunate to have Joshua Bohnsack edit this manuscript. Josh, you pushed me to share my emotionally difficult story in a way that makes sense to readers who haven't shared my cultural experiences.

Thank you, Marie White-Small and Peggy Moran for ably editing early drafts of the manuscript.

Thank you, Anne Greene and Lis Harris for encouraging me to write this story when I attended the Wesleyan Writers Conference with a manuscript idea.

Thank you, James Astrachan for safeguarding my intellectual property.

Thank you, Valerie Cole-James, Veda Pendleton, Liana Brown, Elizabeth Lopez and Felipe Cabrera for reading the manuscript and providing invaluable feedback.

Thank you early endorsers: Dr. Kay Redfield Jamison, Dr. Cassandra Joubert, Mimi Baird, Andrea M. Cole, Nana-Ama Danquah and Dr. Diane Pomerantz.

Thank you for prayerful and/or financial support: Elder Bruce Edwards, Sr. and the congregation at Apostolic Church of Jesus Christ (Glen Burnie, MD,) Allen and Jo Ann Russell, Desiree Barnes, Gloria Penny Mullings, Lela Richardson, Latisha Jackson, Michelle Edwards, Regina Foreman, Tony and Wendy Baysmore, Gwendolyn Williams, Lida Bates, Ellen R. Berhane, Bruk and Amara Berhane, Shanee Johnson, Kenneth Greif, Leslie Ries, Michael and Brandon King, Adam Turnage III, Delores Johnson and my loving sisters at Bible Study Fellowship (Lutherville, MD).

And . . . much love always to my niece, Camryn D. Little, who reminds us all that we CAN get up, because we are NOT defeated!

CHARITA COLE BROWN earned a BA in English from Wesleyan University and an MAT in Early Childhood Education from Towson University in Maryland. She is now retired and lives in Baltimore with her two daughters.